ELIZABETH TAYLOR'S KISS

And Other Brushes with Hollywood

ELIZABETH TAYLOR'S KISS

And Other Brushes with Hollywood

DAVID WOOD

The Book Guild Ltd

First published in Great Britain in 2022 by
The Book Guild Ltd
Unit E2 Airfield Business Park,
Harrison Road, Market Harborough,
Leicestershire. LE16 7UL
Tel: 0116 2792299
www.bookguild.co.uk
Email: info@bookguild.co.uk
Twitter: @bookguild

Typeset in 11pt Minion Pro

Printed and bound by CPI Group (UK) Ltd, Croydon, CR0 4YY

ISBN 978 1914471 902

British Library Cataloguing in Publication Data.
A catalogue record for this book is available from the British Library.

For Jacqui, Katherine and Rebecca

ELIZABETH TAYLOR'S KISS

And Other Brushes with Hollywood

Close encounters with (*in order of appearance*):

Elizabeth Taylor
Richard Burton
Shelley Winters
David Hemmings
Malcolm McDowell
Christopher Plummer
Roger Moore
Anthony Perkins
James Mason
Hayley Mills

Plus full supporting cast…

CONTENTS

INTRODUCTION

My earlier memoir, *Filming If....*, described my unforgettable experience in 1968, as a young actor lucky enough to be selected by the director Lindsay Anderson to play a major role in what was to become an iconic British film. The positive reaction to my book has encouraged me to write about more acting highlights of my career. I have been fortunate enough to work with several movie greats, never as a star, but as a supporting player and as an occasional writer.

My sole visit to Hollywood, in 1990, lasted for five days, during which I experienced raging toothache and my younger daughter's hair turned green. But despite this, my brushes with Hollywood personalities and productions have provided indelible memories throughout my acting and writing career. As a child, growing up in Surrey and later in Sussex, Hollywood meant Disney. I recall crying when Bambi's mother died, and the animated *Cinderella* stayed with me enough to influence my decision, when writing my own version years later, to omit the Buttons character and substitute him as Cinderella's friend with Disney-style mice. Some of the first songs I learned to sing while my father accompanied me on the piano, were from Disney's *Alice in Wonderland*. And when I wrote and produced my first puppet shows at the age of ten, Minnie

Mouse was a featured character. I remember too developing an interest in wildlife, thanks largely to Disney's *The Living Desert* and *The Vanishing Prairie*, which wove together stories with facts about the animal kingdom. Little did I know then that I would in the future have some extraordinary dealings with Disney.

Saturday Morning Cinema was never part of my early life, but in my teens I enjoyed the big Hollywood musicals like *The King and I* and *South Pacific*. And, although I didn't perhaps understand the sexual implications of *Gigi*, I loved the songs. This came in handy when some years later I was asked to sing the title song at my audition for Andrew Lloyd Webber's musical, *Jeeves*. It won me the role of Bingo Little. Seeing the British musicals *Salad Days* and *Oliver!* influenced my subsequent writing more than the Hollywood blockbusters. As for comedy, I preferred British humour like *Carry on Sergeant* to American films like *Some Like It Hot*, which was to appeal more as I grew older. But once we had a television, first rented in time for the Coronation in 1953, the American sitcoms like *I Love Lucy* and *I Married Joan* were unmissable. These included a considerable amount of physical comedy, with the actors shot full-length rather than in close-up (John Cleese was to use a similar technique years later in his *Fawlty Towers*). I think it was the theatricality of this style that appealed to me, as my interest in performing was developing.

At school it was often the films we were considered too young to see that attracted our attention the most. We were not permitted to witness the charms of Brigitte Bardot in *And God Created Woman* or the terror of the Janet Leigh shower scene in *Psycho*. *The Camp on Blood Island* was another forbidden X-rated film in 1958 from Hammer that featured cruelties handed out by the Japanese in a prison camp in Malaya. At the age of fourteen, my friend Patrick and I decided we wanted to see it, and to do so our elaborate plan involved secretly going to see an approved film, *The Vikings*, after school one day, without telling our parents. Then, on the Saturday, we announced to our parents that we were going to see *The Vikings*, at the Odeon, Bognor Regis, but instead went to the matinée of the violent film at the Picturedrome. Returning home, we were able to talk about *The Vikings* from the earlier viewing and our parents never found out the truth. A couple of years later Pat and I were legitimately able to see *Dr. No*, the first James Bond film. I don't think it made much of an impression, because I have never felt inclined to see any subsequent James Bond movies, despite their massive success. And I have never seen a *Star Wars* film, as science fiction has never grabbed me. My writing and adapting have often used fantasy, but I have always favoured stories where the fantasy springs from reality. I loved, and still love, the story of *Peter Pan*, in which the children leave their real life, flying out of the window to the fantasy world of Neverland. Similarly, Roald Dahl's stories, many of which I had the privilege of adapting for the stage, start off 'real' and then take off into fantasy. *The BFG*, *The Witches* and *James and the Giant Peach* are classic examples. Somehow, for me, stories set in an alien world of their own, such as Tolkien's *The Lord of the Rings* and *The Hobbit*, have never had the same appeal.

To fill in time before going to university I managed to find a job at the Theatre Royal, Bognor Regis, a proper small Edwardian theatre that had become a cinema. My main role was as a bingo caller, which I loved. It was to help develop my entertaining skills, and I was even allowed to sing songs and do magic before the bingo started, featuring audience participation with our regular clientele. I was also Assistant House Manager for the monthly wrestling sessions, and when the cinema was operating, I flashed my torch to usher the audience to their seats. This meant I could see the films several times, never all the way through, but in snatches during lulls in my ushering. Particularly memorable was *Mutiny on the Bounty* in 1962, starring Marlon Brando, which played a short summer season to capacity audiences. My favourite memory from the same year, however, concerns *Whatever Happened to Baby Jane?* I always tried to make sure I was in the auditorium for the iconic moment when Bette Davis serves Joan Crawford her supper, lifting the lid of the tureen to reveal dead rats. I loved witnessing the audience let out a collective gasp of disgusted horror.

But none of these experiences made me a devotee of film or a Hollywood movie buff. My subsequent brushes with Hollywood, though highly significant in my career, were certainly not driven by a desire to work there. I never dreamed of stardom as an actor or imagined myself writing for the glamorous world of Tinseltown.

In contrast, my friend Malcolm McDowell, with whom I was fortunate enough to act in Lindsay Anderson's film *If...*, made no secret of the fact that film stardom was his goal. While I went back into repertory theatre acting, he led a spartan life, turning down any work that wasn't a major movie. His remarkable determination paid off when Joseph Losey offered him the co-starring role opposite Robert Shaw in *Figures in a Landscape*. Soon after, he gave his iconic performance in *A Clockwork Orange*, and his career took off. Seven years after *If...* our paths crossed again in Jack Gold's *Aces High*. This gave me a brush with Hollywood that I will recount later in this book.

In the years between *If...* and *Aces High* I was happily acting on stage and on television, usually cast as the best friend or a close relative of the main character. I didn't wish for greater things, and the children's plays I had written were doing gratifyingly well in London and in many regional theatres. During this period, I had two brushes with Hollywood, both of which involved interviews to act in movies. First, I was summoned to the Athenaeum Hotel in Piccadilly to meet an American producer who thought I might be ideal for his production of *Alfred the Great*. He had seen me in *If...*, playing a seventeen-year-old. He said that my fair hair and light skin were perfect for the role he had in mind, but unfortunately I wasn't old enough to play it. For this role he really wanted somebody in their early twenties. I pointed out that I was twenty-five, but he didn't believe me. He seemed more interested in finding out whether I had been on the set during the filming of the nude scene in *If....* than in auditioning me for his film. Needless to say I didn't get the role. A happier interview came when the great Sir Richard Attenborough was looking for someone to play Churchill in *Young Winston*. It was thought that my face showed a passing resemblance to the young Churchill. Sir Richard was extremely friendly and he subsequently sent me a letter of consolation, saying that I had come third in this casting competition. When I saw the film, it was clear that Simon Ward was an ideal choice, and certainly I could never have ridden horses as proficiently as him. MGM produced *Alfred the Great* in 1969 and Columbia produced *Young Winston* in 1972, two Hollywood studios for whom I was destined never to work.

But to return to my 1990 visit to Los Angeles and the one and only real brush with Hollywood, the location – it was part of a family trip to California to meet up with my wife's aunt and cousins. Auntie Joan had been a GI bride. She and three of her grown-up children and grandchildren all lived in Newport Beach. Her fourth child had sadly died a few years earlier. We based ourselves at her home, introducing our daughters, Katherine, fourteen, and Rebecca, nearly eleven, to their American cousins. Our five-day diversion to experience the attractions of Hollywood were at first marred by my wretched toothache. At first I thought it was a recurring sinus problem. Painkillers permitted me to drive from Auntie Joan's to the Mikado Hotel on Riverside Drive, North Hollywood. To reach the hotel's reception we crossed a willow-pattern-style bridge over a pond, the home of several koi carp. The sun shone down from a cloudless sky and the girls enjoyed a dip in the hotel pool. But the next day the relentless ache in my head forced us to abort a drive to Venice Beach. Instead I found a doctor, who confirmed my sinus suspicions and prescribed some pills, which didn't seem to do much good. In a shopping mall we saw an advertisement for the Studio City Dental Group and made an appointment for the next day. Dr Eric Shapiro, who had trained in London, inspired confidence, and eventually discovered, thanks to a panoramic X-ray, a small grey area. His prodding burst an abscess. He then began root canal treatment, saying that all should be fine until I got home, when my own dentist could complete the work. To the family's relief, the pain cleared immediately, so that we were able to drive straight to Butterfields, a picturesque restaurant in the former home of the actor John Barrymore. We were entertained there by Leon Embry, who managed the Los Angeles office of Samuel French, my play publishers. Some of my children's plays were proving quite popular in America, and it was useful to chat to Leon, who gave us a lovely lunch and promised to promote my plays to the community theatre companies on the Samuel French mailing list. Now we busied ourselves seeing the sights. We drove up Rodeo Drive. We went on the Universal Studios tour, where the girls flew the *E.T.* bicycle and rode in the *Back to the Future* car. On Hollywood Boulevard we found a magic shop, where I invested in a new Wilting Flower, one of the features of my Magic and Music Show. And outside Grauman's Chinese Theatre we found Hayley Mills's star, part of the Hollywood Walk of Fame. The previous year Hayley had splendidly starred as the mother in my TV film adaptation of Michelle Magorian's *Back Home*. This was a co-production with the Disney Channel. I had hoped to meet up with the producer Cathy Johnson in her Hollywood office, but this never happened. But we did visit Hayley Carr, the young actress who, aged eleven, had so movingly played Rusty, the elder Hayley's daughter. Young Hayley had come to England for the filming, accompanied by her mother, Doreen. They lived in Glendale, and warmly welcomed us to their home.

After another couple of swims in the Mikado pool, Becky's hair turned an interesting shade of green. Concerned that there might be a toxic mix of chemicals in the pool, we reported the matter to the front desk. But the next day we were visiting Rita and Jonathan

Lynn, who reassured us that this was not an abnormal occurrence. Jonathan, probably best known for co-writing with Antony Jay the brilliant BBC television sitcom *Yes Minister*, had helped my children's writing career hugely by directing two of my plays, the first London production of *The Plotters of Cabbage Patch Corner* and the premiere and Old Vic productions of *The Gingerbread Man*. Now he had carved out a successful career directing movies in Hollywood and a couple of years after our visit he achieved major recognition with *My Cousin Vinny*. It was great to see Jonathan and Rita enjoying their success, in their impressive home in the Hollywood hills, with a fabulous view over Los Angeles and complete with a swimming pool and an imposing Bentley in their long and winding drive.

Despite this family holiday being my only trip to Tinseltown, I realise how fortunate and privileged I was to have met during my life and career such luminaries as Elizabeth Taylor, Richard Burton, Shelley Winters, Roger Moore, Anthony Perkins and David Hemmings. These memorable moments, alongside my dealings with Disney, both abortive and successful, are my brushes with Hollywood described in this book.

David Wood

WHEN HOLLYWOOD CAME TO OXFORD

1966

Dr Faustus starring Richard Burton and Elizabeth Taylor

It was perhaps the most dramatic and tempestuous love affair of the late twentieth century between two great actors: Richard Burton, who had conquered stage and screen with roles such as Henry V and Hamlet, Becket, Jimmy Porter in Look Back in Anger *and Alec Leamas in* The Spy Who Came in from the Cold *– and film goddess Elizabeth Taylor, who had started out aged twelve in* National Velvet *and progressed to stardom in* Cat on a Hot Tin Roof *and* Suddenly Last Summer, *later winning Oscars for* Who's Afraid of Virginia Woolf? *and* BUtterfield 8. *In 1966 their exotic world was about to collide with my less-than-glamorous student days in Oxford.*

At first I thought it was a joke. On 4 November, 1975, a telegram arrived addressed to 'David Wood and friend', at the Stage Door of the Key Theatre, Peterborough, where I was appearing in *Think of a Number*, a musical revue I had co-written.

I opened it in the dressing room and read:

I DO HOPE YOU WILL JOIN ME IN CELEBRATING RICHARD'S 50TH BIRTHDAY AT THE DORCHESTER HOTEL ON MONDAY NOVEMBER 10 AT 8.30PM ORCHID SUITE STOP DRESS FORMAL OR INFORMAL BLUE JEANS OR WHATEVER YOU WISH STOP RSVP C/O MARJORIE LEE THE DORCHESTER LONDON LOVE ELIZABETH BURTON.

If it was a joke, it was an expensive one. I had never received a telegram with so many words, more like a short letter rather than the truncated text usually associated with telegrams.

After several readings I came to the conclusion that the message really had come from Elizabeth Taylor and that I was indeed invited to Richard Burton's fiftieth birthday party. I sent a reply – by letter, not telegram – saying that my wife Jacqui and I would love to come, but that we would be late arriving, having to drive from Peterborough to Park Lane after my evening performance.

Looking back, it was really rather remarkable to receive the telegram invitation, especially considering that I had not seen the Burtons or been in touch with them since 1966, nine years earlier. It was flattering to think that Elizabeth Taylor should have remembered me. The magical, almost surreal, few days we had shared were, and still are, indelibly engraved in my memory. But I could hardly have expected to retain a place in her and Richard's recollection.

It was well after midnight when we reached the opulent Dorchester, by which time the party was in less than full swing. The Orchid Suite was awash with gold decorations. A band played, but I don't remember seeing people dancing. Richard Burton greeted me warmly, and graciously said hello to Jacqui, who hadn't met him before. Richard seemed relaxed and very coherent, as though, despite his reputation, he had not been drinking alcohol. In his mellifluous Welsh tones, he apologised for the fact that Elizabeth had already gone upstairs, probably to bed. From what we could gather, there had been some sort of incident or argument which caused her to leave the party early. Sorry not to see her, we spoke to a few people, though we didn't know many, then left.

The background to this Hollywood moment had its beginnings in 1966 when I was in my final year reading for a Bachelor of Arts degree in English. My long-suffering tutor, the highly respected academic Christopher (now Sir Christopher) Ricks, had become used to the fact that I spent far more time and attention on my university theatre experiences than my academic studies. He was used to essays being late, or apologies being made for missing a tutorial because of an overnight emergency production meeting. He knew that I had set my sights on a theatrical career, and even told me once that it was my interest in performing magic tricks that had swayed him and the interviewing panel to offer me a place at Worcester College, Oxford.

I had felt privileged, as a grammar school boy, to be offered the chance to go to Oxford, but I had never made a secret of the fact that it was the flourishing student theatre scene that was for me the main attraction. In my first two years I crammed in everything from Shakespeare to revue, from Oscar Wilde to cabaret, appearing in the West End and at the Mermaid Theatre, as well as at the Blue Angel nightclub in Berkeley Square. It was generally accepted that in the third year work took precedence over theatre, and I was resigned to that dictum until news came through in the autumn of 1965 that Richard Burton and Elizabeth Taylor intended to come to Oxford to appear in an Oxford University Dramatic Society production of *Dr Faustus* by Christopher Marlowe. They would appear at the Oxford Playhouse for a week, alongside a student cast. The play would be directed by Professor Nevill Coghill, the Oxford don who had been Burton's tutor during the war years when he was at Exeter College. He had directed Burton in an OUDS production of Shakespeare's *Measure for Measure*, in which Burton played Angelo. Burton's Oxford career was cut short when he was called up to the RAF, but he always retained an admiration for Coghill, and gratitude for his encouragement. Now, as a magnificent gesture of thanks, he and his wife had agreed to perform in *Dr Faustus* to help raise money for the University Theatre Workshop Fund. For a while, we students didn't quite believe that this plan would come to fruition, and, as my third year began, I was resigned to the fact that in any case I would not be involved – but on 29 November a postcard arrived in my college pigeonhole, from Nevill Coghill. He wrote:

Dear David, I hope you will play Wagner in Dr Faustus. *We begin rehearsals on 3 January, 1966 at 10am in the Playhouse. Can I count on your being there? Yours, Nevill Coghill*

What an offer! How on earth could I refuse? I explained the situation in a note to Christopher Ricks, bleating, 'I can't not do this, can I?!'

A typically generous reply came back saying: 'Dear David, Obviously it would be wrong for you not to take part in *Dr Faustus* – a

13

unique opportunity and I hope you'll do very well out of it.' However he continued, very fairly, 'But please let me add that you really must do as much work as possible during all the rest of the time. You never know what long-term life will be like, and it would be as well for you to have a respectable degree. So do a lot of work. I've spoken to the Provost, and he concurs. Yours, Christopher Ricks'. Phew! I replied to Professor Coghill with heartfelt thanks and a big YES, PLEASE!

News filtered through about Professor Coghill's other casting decisions. They included Bob Scott, my great friend and fellow cabaret performer, who was President of OUDS. We had acted together in *Hang Down Your Head and Die* in Oxford and the West End, and he played Bottom when I was Puck in the OUDS open-air production of *A Midsummer Night's Dream* at Stratford-upon-Avon. Bob was to play Chorus and also understudy Richard Burton. Andreas Teuber, an American student, was to play Mephistophilis, and Maria Aitken and Dick Durden-Smith were cast as the Good and Evil Angels. Jacqueline Harvey was to choreograph and Nicholas Young was to be the Assistant Director. For me the best news was that my girlfriend Sheila Dawson was to be one of the dancers and would also understudy Elizabeth Taylor. I was twenty-one. Sheila was nineteen. To all us undergraduates it seemed extraordinary that Burton, then forty, and Taylor, then thirty-three, would risk their reputations on sharing the stage with us. They were at the height of their renown, courting as much media interest as a royal couple. Burton, we were told, had always wanted to play Faustus. Taylor was making her very first stage appearance, albeit in the non-speaking role of Helen of Troy. Ever since starring in *National Velvet* at the age of twelve, Elizabeth Taylor had been regarded as a fine screen actress. She had won an Oscar for *BUtterfield 8*, as well as receiving accolades for *Cat on a Hot Tin Roof* and *Suddenly Last Summer*. Richard Burton had also achieved fame in films including *The Robe*, *My Cousin Rachel* and *Look Back in Anger*, but to British audiences he was most revered for his stage work at Stratford and the Old Vic, playing many Shakespearean roles, including Hamlet, Coriolanus, Prince Hal and even Sir Toby Belch. Perhaps it was not surprising that the British press criticised him for selling out to Hollywood and, when it was announced that he would be playing Faustus, who sold his soul to the Devil, they couldn't resist making comparisons between the character and the actor. Furthermore, the scandalous affair between Burton and Taylor during the filming of *Cleopatra* in 1961–62 had proved a salacious gift for the tabloid press. But now they were married, still pursued by paparazzi, and stars of the gossip columns as much as the silver screen. And they were heading to Oxford to work with a bunch of students. Amazing.

The Christmas vacation arrived. I received a card depicting the medieval sculpture over the entrance to Merton College. It contained the message:

> *Dear David, Delighted to have you as Wagner. Your first mood is impish. Your last is grave. In your first scene with your yellow hair – don't cut it – in your last, the same hair, but powdered white. So glad you found my Chaucer books helpful.* The Masque of Hope – *that forgotten masterpiece! – was great fun. The Princess was seen to laugh. Best Xmas wishes, Nevill Coghill. PS Good luck to your cabaret! My love to Bob.*

Coghill, of course, had written a definitive translation of Chaucer's *The Canterbury Tales*, which was published by Penguin. I must have boldly thanked him for this helpful book. Not only that, I had appeared in a stage version of Coghill's *The Canterbury Tales* at the Oxford Playhouse the previous year. I had first met him then, in somewhat different circumstances. *The Masque of Hope* was a play Coghill wrote. It was performed in 1948 in the University College Quad, before Princess Elizabeth. Directed by Glynne Wickham, the cast included future luminaries Robert Hardy, Tony Richardson, John Schlesinger and Kenneth Tynan. In his postscript, Coghill was kind to mention the cabaret that Bob and I were performing with our partner and my co-writer, John Gould. Our comedy song act was seen at Oxford Balls, the Union, as well as occasionally in Cambridge and London.

Opening Night of *Dr Faustus* was announced as 14 February, 1966. Rehearsals began as planned on 3 January, organised by Peter Wiles and Jane Wilford, two experienced student stage managers. Every afternoon, and some evenings, we would assemble in rehearsal rooms at Balliol, Hertford, and my own college, Worcester, where the gently spoken Nevill Coghill carefully blocked the scenes and enthusiastically offered characterisation guides. His approach was not overtly academic. He was a true man of the theatre. I had attended some of his lectures about Shakespeare, and much enjoyed how he explained Shakespeare's stagecraft as much as his poetry. Once a scene had been staged, sometimes Coghill would hand over to Nick Young, his assistant. Meanwhile Jackie Harvey rehearsed the movement, Andreas ironed out his natural American accent, and David McIntosh developed his powerfully devilish voice as Lucifer. As Wagner, Faustus's servant, I enjoyed preparing to address the audience with my 'I think my master means to die shortly...' speech.

Some of us were sent up to London for costume fittings at the famous Berman's in Shaftesbury Avenue. We met the genial designer, Hutchinson Scott, whose name I had often seen in West End theatre programmes. He was one of the few professionals employed on the production. He designed both set and costumes. Kenneth Jones, a respected musician and conductor, was engaged as composer of the music. And Michael Werner, an artist and sculptor, created ornate masks for the Seven Deadly Sins.

All that was missing in these opening rehearsal weeks was the presence of our two stars. Burton and Taylor were not arriving, we were told, until the end of January. So Bob and Sheila, their understudies, were rehearsed thoroughly as Faustus and Helen.

The idea was that, by the time the Burtons arrived, we would be at a complete run-through stage, which they could watch, before being slotted in, as it were. Burton clearly respected Coghill so much that he trusted in his judgement and directing skills.

On Monday, 31 January, exactly two weeks before opening night, the Burtons flew into Heathrow from Los Angeles. 'Only the red carpet was missing,' reported the *Daily Express*, noting that, 'immigration and customs officials obligingly walked 100 yards to the lounge from the arrivals channels to clear the Burtons ... They were driven straight from the aircraft, and without going through normal controls were taken to the Ambassador Lounge'. The *Daily Sketch* seemed more interested in Richard Burton's beard than Elizabeth Taylor's mink coat. He had grown it for *Dr Faustus*, and would keep it for Zeffirelli's *The Taming of the Shrew*, which was to be filmed with both the Burtons later in the year. They had been married for nearly two years now, and had become something of a double act.

The following day, they rolled into Oxford, literally, in their splendid green Rolls-Royce, driven by Gaston Sanz, their loyal chauffeur and bodyguard. After lunch with Nevill Coghill, we all saw them in the flesh for the first time. They were gracious and glamorous. The *Daily Mail* announced, 'the most publicised three weeks in Oxford University's 700-year history began yesterday.' Suddenly the whole thing seemed real. We all trooped off to the ballroom of Oxford's most famous hotel, the Randolph, and performed a run-through of the play. The Burtons watched with concentration and no hint of condescension. Bob and Sheila must have been nervous acting out the roles that would eventually be played by the Burtons, but all seemed to go well. I remember Burton made a self-deprecating comment that, having seen Bob in the role, his presence wasn't really necessary. Sheila was introduced to Elizabeth, who officially approved her as her understudy. I had the chance of exchanging a few words with her, and was immediately hypnotised by her warm smile and friendliness. She joked that she knew every line of her non-speaking role. Burton told us that he knew his part, but not as well as he thought he did. He said that, when working through them, a lot of Marlowe's lines had started coming out as Burton's lines!

When rehearsals started the next day, it became clear that Burton had indeed done his homework. Although he used a script, he used it more for writing notes than as an aide-memoire. At first he spoke quietly, unemphatically, but his characteristically melodic tones were excitingly apparent. Work took place in the Oxford Police Station gymnasium in St Aldate's, chosen for its security and privacy. No press or photographers were allowed in, apart from a student reporter from *Cherwell*, the university newspaper.

Burton's calm concentration involved a lot of smoking. Whenever he felt the need to light up, he placed a hand over his shoulder, whereupon the trusty Gaston would approach, place a cigarette between his outstretched fingers, then light it from behind.

Coghill, then aged sixty-six, directed Burton quietly yet enthusiastically. Burton rarely questioned his blocking or interpretation. He was quoted as saying, 'he is as near to a saint as any man I know'. A few amendments were insisted upon. No actor was allowed to get too close to him. Perhaps he knew he needed a magic circle of space around him to portray his power. Roger Sherman was playing the Old Man who attempts at the last moment to persuade Faustus of the error of his ways. Sherman wrote to me:

> *Coghill had asked me to fall on my knees in supplication – well, descend to ground level as an Old Man might – and grasp Faustus around the knees. I did this for the first time to the then greatest living Welshman, who, to my mortification, shrank away in horror. What had I done wrong? I checked for hang-nails; had I exacerbated an old rugby injury? Burton stormed over to the*

director: 'Nevill, I said to you from the start, no one in the cast can
touch me physically, please change this!' So the upshot was that the
Old Man descended to the floor in front of Faustus in an attitude
of prayer, and the Burton knees remained sacrosanct.

The scenes between Faustus and Mephistophilis, even early on in rehearsal, seemed pretty impressive. Andreas's persuasive other-worldliness gave Burton a solid presence against which to play, which seemed to ignite a spark of urgent passion.

For the first few days Elizabeth was apparently unwell, so didn't attend rehearsal. This meant that Sheila found herself acting Helen of Troy in the famous 'Is this the face that launched a thousand ships' scene, and acquitted herself well.

After rehearsal we sometimes accompanied Burton to the Apollo pub across the road. He seemed very relaxed over a pint of bitter. It must have been a relief that there were no paparazzi clicking away, and that the pub regulars took little or no notice of him. He took no chances, however. Gaston came too, and never kept his eyes off him, even escorting him to the gents. Gaston paid for our drinks. We had already noticed that Burton, like royalty, never carried anything in the pockets of his camel jacket. Gaston looked after the cash and the cigarettes. At one point a photographer came in and was granted a shot, but Burton, clearly from experience, made quite sure that he was surrounded by us undergraduates, both male and female, in such a way that the photo couldn't be cropped to imply he was privately entertaining one young lady.

Later that week, Elizabeth came to rehearsal. Afterwards she came to the pub with Richard and a group of us. Simply dressed in black slacks and jumper, wearing the minimum of make-up, she chatted to us in a happy and relaxed way. I found myself sitting at her feet. She noticed that I was wearing an old sweater, with my elbows poking out from frayed holes. A typical student sweater. I suppose I thought it was arty. 'You can't go around like that!'

laughed Elizabeth. 'Richard's got lots of sweaters. I'll bring you one.' The next day she brought me two, one beige and one a burgundy colour. One even had 'Beverly Hills' on the label. Whether or not Richard knew that his wardrobe had been raided, I'll never know. But it was a very kind gesture. I don't think I ever wore them, but maybe it is significant that I still have them, souvenirs of an unforgettable encounter.

Most of us students were, I'm sure, dazzled by our admittance to the fringes of celebrity that the Burtons seemed ready to share with us. They genuinely seemed to enjoy our company. We all felt a bit special, as a little of the glamour rubbed off onto us. Or perhaps it was the other way round. Perhaps the Burtons enjoyed entering our world of comparative normality for a while. Though still protected by their entourage – not only Gaston, but assorted agents and managers, hair and make-up artists, and a secretary – in Oxford perhaps they didn't feel so hounded by press and constantly exposed to unwelcome scrutiny.

Sheila and I may have been luckier than most, partly because of Sheila's understudying duties. I remember one afternoon going to collect her from the Burtons' suite at the Randolph. Girlish giggles greeted me. I discovered Sheila and Elizabeth like excited schoolgirls, kneeling at a dressing table. Elizabeth was handing Sheila priceless jewels to try on. A necklace, some earrings. Elizabeth wasn't showing off her possessions, rather enjoying the fun of a dressing-up game.

On another occasion Sheila and I were invited to dinner with the Burtons, just the four of us, in the dining room of the Bear Hotel in nearby town Woodstock. Richard and Elizabeth had a suite at this hotel too. The Randolph was mainly for meetings and somewhere to relax during rehearsals. The Bear was where they slept. On the day of our dinner I had a second costume fitting in London, so it was arranged that Gaston would pick me up from the station and then drive Sheila and me to Woodstock in the Rolls-Royce. We certainly felt very privileged, though our youth and inexperience made us take this taste of luxurious living in our stride. We may have felt nervous, dining in a posh hotel with two such icons, but it all seemed to go well. Maybe it is no surprise that I can remember nothing of what we ate or what we talked about. As Gaston drove us back to Oxford, the evening felt like a surreal dream. Gaston, we discovered, had looked after Elizabeth long before Burton arrived on the scene. This kind, squat Basque in dark glasses had apparently seen service in the Free French Commandos during the war. He wore small ribbons on his jacket awarded for his bravery. He clearly worshipped Elizabeth. We were told that he had often protected her from paparazzi, who would lie in wait in underground car parks. He was a judo black belt, who would stand no nonsense. A huge admirer of Winston Churchill, he had brought his cine-camera to film footage at Churchill's birthplace in nearby Blenheim Palace and at his grave in Bladon. We appreciated his courtesy and safe driving. Rather unfairly he was nicknamed Oddjob by the press and some of the students.

Other members of the Burton entourage we met included Ron Berkeley, Richard's affable make-up man, and Bob Wilson, his smartly dressed, quietly spoken valet and dresser. We regularly saw the Burtons' agent, the urbane John Heyman, who had also co-produced Burton's celebrated *Hamlet* on Broadway in 1964. A few years later, Heyman produced Joseph Losey's classic film *The Go-Between*. His wife, Norma, also became a film producer. With *The Honorary Consul* (1983), she became the first British woman to singlehandedly produce an independent feature film. Their son, David, grew up to produce all the *Harry Potter* films. Running around doing a lot of the donkey work was John Heyman's assistant, Morgan Reece-Williams, an earnest young Welshman.

By the end of the first week, Sheila and I had become wrapped up in our dreamlike wander through wonderland. Rehearsals were proceeding well and neither of us had attempted any academic work. The Burtons had, in those few days, taken over our lives. It was a uniquely special time, yet Richard and Elizabeth had somehow made our participation in their rarefied world both natural and enjoyable. I wrote a card to my mother and stepfather: 'The excitement continues – they both are very charming and sweet – very relaxed and natural – and she is very intelligent I think – Sheila has rehearsed the Helen scene with him several times!! D.' I was clearly bewitched!

On the Tuesday of the second week, only six days before opening night, we were reminded – and how – of the colossal interest the production of *Dr Faustus* was generating. We were all asked to attend the press conference, which took place on the Playhouse stage. A sea of journalists and photographers greeted us, plus television cameras. The stalls looked almost full. Sheila and I sat downstage right. Bob, as president of OUDS, hosted the event, standing downstage left. Sitting at a table in the centre of the stage sat Burton and Taylor. They were quite casually dressed, he in a light-coloured cardigan, she in black slacks and a fur wrap. They spoke into a microphone. Richard graciously acknowledged Coghill. 'I thought since Professor Coghill started me off,' he said, 'I should finish him off.' He appeared to flatter us undergraduate actors by saying that he preferred this Oxford to the one he had known, because there were more talented people about now. He said he had wanted to play Faustus for twenty years, that the speech towards the end, when Faustus begs for his soul, was the greatest in English drama. He also announced his hope that the play might be filmed, using the same student cast. This would also be in aid of the workshop fund. One reporter asked if he had ever thought of joining the National Theatre. This seemed to be a dig at the fact that Burton had abandoned classical theatre for Hollywood. Richard spoke of Olivier, who ran the National Theatre, as a great friend. He said he had been asked to play Falstaff and other parts, but had

Me, centre, aged ten, with my puppet show helpers, Bruce and David.

My daughters, Katherine and Rebecca, looking at Hayley Mills's Walk of Fame paving stone outside Grauman's Chinese Theatre in Hollywood.

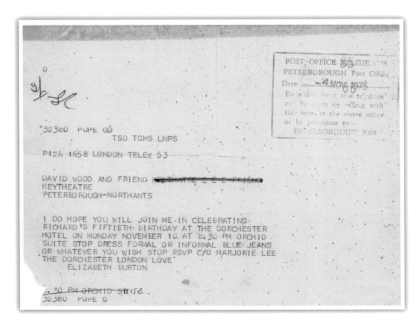

The 1975 telegram invitation from Elizabeth Taylor.

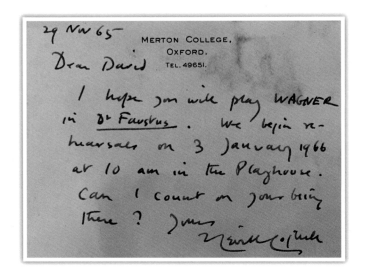

Dr Faustus: *Professor Nevill Coghill invites me to play Wagner.*

Dr Faustus: *Oxford Playhouse – a wide
shot of the* Dr Faustus *press conference.*

Dr Faustus: *Oxford Playhouse – the press conference.
Sitting left are Nicholas Young, Sheila Dawson and me.
Bob Scott is extreme right, with beard and glasses.*

Dr Faustus: *After the press conference. L to R – me, Nicholas Young, Sheila Dawson, Richard Heffer, unknown, Richard Burton, Hugh Williams, Elizabeth Taylor, Nevill Coghill, Jacqueline Harvey, Andreas Teuber.*

Dr Faustus: *L to R – Elizabeth Taylor, Nicholas Young and me.*

Dr Faustus: *The Burton sweaters – a gift from Elizabeth Taylor. And the Beverly Hills label!*

Dr Faustus: *Acting notes from Nevill Coghill.*

Dr Faustus: *The programme cover.*

THE TRAGICAL HISTORY OF DR. FAUSTUS

CAST

· Dr. Faustus	RICHARD BURTON
Helen of Troy	ELIZABETH TAYLOR
· Chorus	ROBERT SCOTT (Merton) understudying *Faustus*
· Mephistophilis	ANDREAS TEUBER (St. John's)
Evil Angel	RICHARD DURDEN-SMITH (Merton) understudying *Mephistophilis*
Good Angel	MARIA AITKEN (St. Anne's)
· Wagner	DAVID WOOD (Worcester)
· Valdes	RICHARD CARWARDINE (Corpus Christi)
· Cornelius	RAM CHOPRA (Oriel) understudying *The Emperor*
· 1st Scholar	RICHARD HEFFER (St. Peter's)
· 2nd Scholar	HUGH WILLIAMS (Jesus)
· 3rd Scholar	GWYDION THOMAS (Magdalen)
· Lucifer	DAVID MCINTOSH (Christ Church)
Beelzebub	JEREMY ECCLES (Jesus)
· Pride	NICHOLAS GRAY (Keble)
· Envy	ANTONY BRAIME (Merton)
· Wrath	MICHAEL MENEAUGH (Lincoln)
· Covetousness	PHILLIP HODSON (St. Peter's)
· Gluttony	ALAN MOSES (University)
· Sloth	PATRICK BARWISE (Lincoln)
· Lechery	JENNY MOSS (St. Hugh's)
The Pope	RICHARD CARWARDINE
The Cardinal	NICHOLAS LOUKES (Christ Church)
The Emperor	IAN MARTER (S.E.H.) understudying *Chorus*
A Knight	DAVID JESSEL (Merton)
A Horse-courser	SEBASTIAN WALKER (New College)
A Clown	RICHARD HARRISON (New College)
Duke of Vanholt	RICHARD ALFORD (Keble)
Duchess of Vanholt	ELIZABETH O'DONOVAN (St. Hugh's)
Robin	ANDREW HILTON (New College)
Ralph	SIMON TAYLOR (St. John's)
Vintner	BRUCE ALEXANDER (New College)
An Old Man	ROGER SHERMAN (Hertford)
Demon Wife	SUSAN WATSON (Somerville)
Acrobats	PETER LYNCH (St. Catherine's) and JOHN SANDBACH (St. John's)
Dancers	JACQUELINE HARVEY (L.M.H.), CAROLYN BENNITT (L.M.H.), MARY FAIRBOTHAM (L.M.H.), HAZEL NEARY (L.M.H.), SHEILA PESKITT (L.M.H.), SHEILA DAWSON (Ruskin) understudying *Helen of Troy*, SYLVIA GILPIN (St. Antony's), MARIAN HARLAND (Somerville)
Lady-in-Waiting	PETRONELLA PULSFORD (St. Hilda's)
Friar	GEOFFREY NICE (Keble) understudying *Evil Angel*
Trumpeters	BRIAN KENNEDY (Lincoln), RODNEY LORD (Christ Church)
Organist	ROBERT BOTTONE (Christ Church)

The *Dancers* and *Deadly Sins* will also play as *Friars and Demons, Courtiers*, etc.

Production Designer: Hutchinson Scott. *Associate*: Peter Beard. *Costumes designed* by Hutchinson Scott
Music composed by Kenneth Victor Jones. *Masks for the Seven Deadly Sins* by Michael Werner
Assistant Director: Nicholas Young. *Choreographer*: Jacqueline Harvey

DIRECTED BY NEVILL COGHILL

Dr Faustus: *The cast list.*

Dr Faustus: *Faustus and Mephistophilis.*

Dr Faustus: *Helen of Troy.*

Dr Faustus: *Faustus with students.*

W. S. G. Productions

Patrons: Richard Burton and Elizabeth Taylor

DAVID WOOD
BOB SCOTT
JOHN GOULD

Dr Faustus: *The prestigious letterhead!*

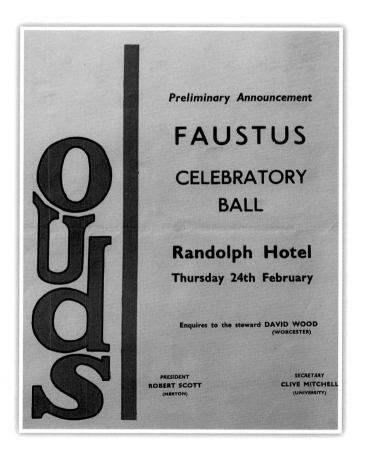

Dr Faustus: *Did this event actually happen?*

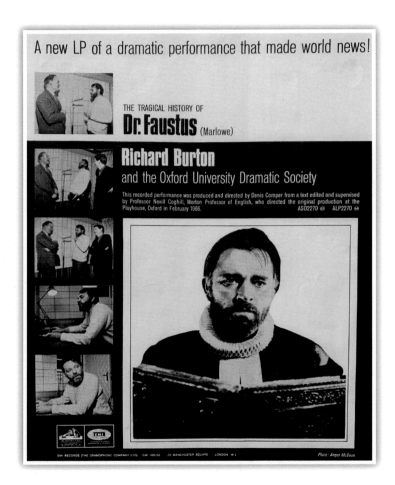

Dr Faustus: *Magazine advert for the LP recording.*

Dr Faustus: *When Hollywood came to Oxford.*

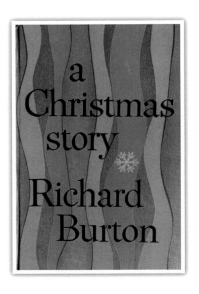

Dr Faustus: *Richard Burton's* A Christmas Story
– a gift from my stepfather.

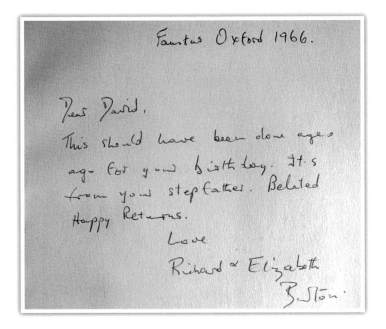

Faustus Oxford 1966.

Dear David,
This should have been done ages
ago for your birthday. It's
from your stepfather. Belated
Happy Returns.
            Love
            Richard & Elizabeth
                        Burton.

Dr Faustus: *The Richard Burton dedication in* A Christmas Story.

never been able to find the time. But he did say that, in a few years' time, he would like to play Lear, once he had gained a bit more weight. At this point, Elizabeth, who had so far said very little, leaned towards Richard and whispered in his ear. Richard reported that she had offered him some of her weight. This was a reference to the fact that they had only recently finished filming *Who's Afraid of Virginia Woolf?*, for which Elizabeth had, for artistic reasons, put on extra pounds.

Elizabeth maintained a jokey attitude throughout the press conference, saying that as Helen 'all I do is kiss Richard and move around.' She said she thought she should appear masked from head to foot, because it wasn't easy to show a face that would launch a thousand ships. Her determination not to take herself too seriously was appealing and diplomatic.

The *Sun* newspaper, perhaps surprisingly, reported a bit of Burton philosophy when he was asked if he thought the part was appropriate in his case. 'Everybody is offered a choice: one easy, one difficult. Most men, regardless of their craft, profession or background, are faced at one time or another with an obvious, easy one and a difficult, more rewarding one.' Quite what Richard was implying with this statement, I'm not sure.

Terry Coleman, reporting in the *Guardian*, took a more satirical view of the proceedings: 'the press conference had got off to a precarious start,' he wrote. 'Police and press regarded each other closely. Miss Sheila Dawson, Helen's understudy, took care to be photographed with Mrs Burton, sharing a joke, as they say.' A little unkind. He smiled, too, at the idea of Elizabeth Taylor playing a non-speaking role. 'Wasn't she, asked a reporter, afraid that someone of her stature, in so small a part, might unbalance the play just drifting around in long robes? She hoped not. "Ah," said Burton, after a glance at her, "but she'll unbalance me, I'll tell you."' Such gentle jokes at each other's expense were typical of the Burtons. They enjoyed teasing one another. I always felt that they were comfortable in each other's presence, and enjoyably 'normal' in their relationship. Certainly that was the impression they gave in Oxford. It was a shame when a few years later the relationship soured.

Terry Coleman also had a go at Bob, as host: 'Mr Bob Scott, President of the Oxford University Dramatic Society, set about running things his way. "Only one more minute," he admonished photographers. They glowered. The general opinion was that Mr Scott should go far, the farther the better. An agency man said he'd had less trouble at Buck Palace.'

Overall, the press conference was a civilised affair. Although some members of the press may have wanted to reflect a cynical attitude towards the whole enterprise, I sensed an overriding respect and a wish to show appreciation for Burton and Taylor's magnanimous gesture.

We students were not of particular interest to the press, although Sheila, as Elizabeth's attractive understudy, was photographed and interviewed, particularly in the local papers. The *Oxford Mail*, soon after the Burtons' arrival in the city, printed a photo with the heading, 'LIZ TAYLOR'S UNDERSTUDY: I'M THRILLED'. Incidentally, Richard never ever called Elizabeth 'Liz'. And he was annoyed if anyone else did. And I never heard Elizabeth call Richard 'Dick'.

On one occasion some of us shared the media spotlight. Kenneth Allsop, the television reporter, interviewed several of us for the BBC *Tonight* programme. I fancy we were all quite gushing in our excitement, though I like to think we portrayed for the television camera a cool appreciation of our good fortune.

Not long after the press conference we moved into the theatre for technical rehearsals. I had wondered what accommodation the Burtons and their team would appropriate backstage. The Playhouse dressing rooms were small and there were not many of them. I needn't have worried. The Burtons used their suite at the Randolph to prepare. A special route was created for them to go straight to the stage of the adjacent Playhouse, by being escorted through the covered hotel car park, down a short alleyway and into the side of the theatre. There were always a few policemen outside patrolling the perimeter of the theatre and guarding the stage door.

I don't recall the technical rehearsals in much detail. We were all encouraged, if not ordered, not to go into the auditorium to watch proceedings when we were not performing ourselves. So we remained backstage while the production took shape and sound and lighting were added. We could hear the proceedings through the dressing-room tannoys, but by now we all knew the play quite well, so didn't spend our time with ears glued to the speakers.

My own scenes must have passed without too much incident. I remember getting used to the trap door that had been carved into the stage to accommodate Faustus's magic book. And I remember, though didn't witness, the chaos that reigned in the Seven Deadly Sins' scene, when it was suddenly plunged into blackout, in order to see the effect of their specially created luminous costumes.

Kept in confinement backstage, we never actually saw the eagerly anticipated Helen of Troy scene. Elizabeth's costume had been specially designed by Irene Sharaff, her regular costume designer. It was ornate and glamorous, with a hairdo to match, and probably looked incongruously different in style from Hutchinson Scott's designs. But I suppose that was the whole point. Helen was from a different world, perhaps from the world of Faustus's imagination. She became a fantasy, a phantom bathed in dry ice. But we never saw it. Except Maria Aitken, who played the Good Angel and had finished her role by the interval. 'At the dress rehearsal we were told we couldn't go out and watch from the auditorium, but I was determined to see Elizabeth Taylor make her entrance as Helen of Troy,' she wrote to me. 'I crouched in the Circle, seeing myself as the witty cynical reporter to the rest of the cast. It seemed promising material – Miss Taylor was wearing a short white toga, white satin winkle-pickers and about 20lbs of false hair. She teetered on in a cloud of dry ice towards Richard Burton. Now remember, these two were the most famous lovers in the world, trampling their spouses to get together, reviled by the press, adored by the public. Well, her get-up was a travesty, but the two of them utterly transcended all that! And I can honestly say that when they kissed it was the single most electrifying moment I have ever seen in well over half a century of theatre-going.'

Just before opening night, I received a hand-written postcard from Nevill Coghill:

Dear David, A new point. 1) Your first entry. Give a slight start followed by a glimmer of cunning when you see Faustus with his book, at the secret trap door which you hadn't known existed. You have caught him at some secret ploy which excites you (BUT DON'T OVERDO IT). 2) Your third entry (clown scene) Make straight for the trap (but furtively) to see what book it is that your master keeps in so secret a place: lift trap and take it out. Then carry on as before but with delight at your discovery that it is MAGIC (not merely filthy pictures). At the end of the scene, when you get offstage, be sure to hand the book to Peter Wiles or whoever is looking after props, so that the book may be put back into the trap, ready for the next performance. I have run out of proper envelopes. Best wishes, Nevill

Ever the practical director.

Opening night was on 14 February, St Valentine's Day. The *New York Herald Tribune* reported that 'the audience gave the Burtons fifteen curtain calls and nine minutes of applause'. I remember Nevill Coghill being brought onstage to great acclaim.

Detailed recollections of the opening night, and, indeed, the subsequent performances, escape me. Presumably my scenes took place without any hiccups. And there were no reports of people forgetting lines or scenery misbehaving. There were rumours that Bob Wilson regularly stood in the wings, carrying a glass of whisky and a lit cigarette: from time to time Richard would walk offstage for a quick swig and drag. And apparently Elizabeth was escorted by members of the entourage to her entrance upstage left, from where she would enter and slowly cross to downstage right, by which time the entourage had hurried round backstage to meet her in the wings, sometimes with a glass of gin and tonic on a satin cushion. The audience did truly gasp when they saw Elizabeth. Jenny Moss, who played Lechery, wrote to me, 'I learned that the secret of Elizabeth Taylor's glowing make-up and smooth skin was ordinary Johnson's Baby Powder – rubbed into the skin it gives a subtle matt sheen.' Alas, like most of us, I never witnessed the memorable appearance in the flesh.

After each performance, the Burtons would host a reception in their suite at the Randolph. Sheila and I were fortunate enough to be invited regularly. The guests included members of the Burton family, including Ivor, his brother, whose wife was a delightfully homely and chatty lady called Gwen. Other Welsh guests arrived. We were thrilled to meet Harry Secombe and Stanley Baker. I also remember talking to Harvey Orkin, the American writer who was also one of Burton's agents, whose face was familiar from his witty contributions to *Not So Much a Programme, More a Way of Life,* the television programme produced by Ned Sherrin.

Nick Gray, who played Pride, reminded me that on one occasion Richard regaled the guests, in his unique, unforgettable voice, with the poem 'Chapel Deacon' by Welsh poet R.S. Thomas. It's the one with the memorable first line, 'Who put that crease in your soul, Davies?' Burton's reason for reciting this particular poem may have been the presence at the party of Gwydion Thomas, the poet's son, who was in *Dr Faustus,* playing the 3rd Scholar.

The national press unsurprisingly showed much more interest in the opening night of *Dr Faustus* than an average Oxford

University stage production. The editor of the *Daily Mirror* decided that a huge photo should dominate its front page, with the headline, 'The face that launched a students' play'.

Other newspapers and their critics seemed uncertain whether to treat the production as a serious piece of theatre or to review it as a novelty. Felix Barker in the *Evening News* wrote, 'Really it was one of those extravagant, faintly absurd evenings that called for a satirist rather than a critic.' Philip Hope-Wallace in the *Guardian* was kinder: 'Too much advance publicity always induces despondency in a first night's audience. But there was a great sense of occasion at the Oxford Playhouse last night.' Fergus Cashin in the *Daily Sketch* focused on the uniqueness of the night:

> *We were to see the highest paid stars in the universe – Richard Burton and Elizabeth Taylor – act for the first time together in the breathing flesh. And indeed the magic started when they came together and lips met lips in loving kisses towards the end. It was worth waiting for. Throughout, Burton as Faustus was magnificently restrained. He was generous – a first violin playing on a single string: a student prince. But when Elizabeth appeared and the rest departed and silence was broken by fluttering fingers in choc boxes, he lifted his beautiful voice to heaven, and his face and fingers acted. He was glorious. And Elizabeth, without a word to say, decorated the stage as no woman ever has or ever will. 'Heaven is in these lips,' said Burton. And nobody disbelieved him.*

Not all the critics described Burton's performance so glowingly. Bernard Levin in the *Daily Mail* snapped: 'Once upon a time, Mr Burton played Hamlet with as much promise as has been in England since the war, but that was a dozen years ago. It's wonderful what a regimen of rotten films will do.' Ouch. Penelope Gilliatt in the *Observer* was condescending: 'Even if Richard Burton seemed to be unaccountably walking through the part, it was moving and exciting to see him onstage again … if only he had extended himself properly in a better play. Most of *Dr Faustus* is hallowed trash.' Interestingly, the paper's sub-editor had chosen the words 'hallowed trash' as the headline above the review, making it look as though Gilliatt was writing of Burton's performance and the production, rather than commenting on Marlowe's play.

Alan Brien in the *Sunday Telegraph*, under the headline 'Burton scaled down', wrote:

> *Almost any other star but Richard Burton would have seized the spotlight with his lion-cub good looks, his muscular fencer's physique, his resonant, ringing, hunting-field voice, and left the amateurs mowing and muttering in the shadows. But, with what seems to me misplaced generosity, he has scaled himself down to a stolid, sedentary, bespectacled, provincial dominie, celebrating a windfall of Premium Bonds with a jaunt round the tourist traps of Elizabethan Europe.*

'Our Drama Critic' in *The Times* went for the jugular, coupled with a waspish sarcasm:

> *… a sad example of university drama at its worst … Mr Burton's Faustus starts promisingly as a tubby, sedentary figure who discreetly turns the first soliloquy towards comedy: and his opening dialogues with Mephistophilis (Andreas Teuber) have some tension. But thereafter it develops no further. Mr Burton seems to be walking through the part, and his contribution to the stiff high jinks in the Vatican are almost as embarrassing as those of the undergraduate actors. Those who visit the production to see Miss Taylor as a speechless apparition of Helen of Troy will not be out of the theatre before 10.45pm.*

David Nathan in the *Sun* reacted similarly, writing tongue-in-cheek:

> *It was all slightly mad in the best Oxford tradition. Richard Burton, scraggily bearded, bespectacled as becomes a scholar, a fine actor not seen on an English stage for ten years, turns up out of sentiment to do* Dr Faustus *with amateurs at the Oxford Playhouse. A million dollars' worth of Elizabeth Taylor, white and gold, and billowing and bosomy, flits plump and stately across the stage as a vision of Helen of Troy, casts him a longing glance and returns, seconds later, rising slowly from a trap door. They kiss to swelling, sonorous organ music, and the face that launched a thousand films has done her bit for a new workshop for the Oxford University Dramatic Society.*

But Harold Hobson, in the *Sunday Times*, was far less cynical:

> *… the two most celebrated players to be found on any stage in Britain or America … that Mr Burton and Elizabeth Taylor, should, as all the world knows, have been willing to break the rhythm of their careers, in order to appear, for the benefit of the OUDS, as Faustus and Helen of Troy, is one of the finest and most generous compliments ever paid to a university.*

He then gives unequivocal praise to Burton's performance:

> *Mr Burton thrillingly marks the three stages of Faustus's damnation, casually embarking on forbidden knowledge in a universal scholar's light-hearted contempt for all knowledge that is permitted; then smoothly and gaily accommodating himself to Marlowe's worldly jests; finally, in an ecstasy of poetry, at first drunk with admiration as the marvellous beauty of Miss Taylor incarnates Troy's miraculous destroyer, and then electric in agony as he sees Christ's blood streaming in the firmament outside the reach of his imploring hand. The terrified pleading with which he speaks the words,*

'Oh if my soul must suffer for my sin,
Impose some end for my incessant pain'

– is matched by the dazzled and dazzling skill with which he makes
'was this the face that launch'd a thousand ships?' seem like a cry of
wonder we have never heard before.

Not quite as ornately admiring, but genuinely complimentary, were three heavyweight critics. 'Mr Burton's Faustus is very good indeed,' wrote B.A. Young in the *Financial Times*. 'He is well able to match "the mighty line" with a poetic and heroic delivery, which is only slightly spoilt with a tendency to drop his voice at the end of phrases and to insert an automatic pause into a line to emphasise a following word.' W.A. Darlington in the *Daily Telegraph*, under the headline, 'Burton rises to best in Faustus', said, 'Mr Burton's voice is as fine and resonant as ever, and he rose to his best moments when they came.' And Philip Hope-Wallace in the *Guardian* thought that 'Mr Burton will surely carry the play forward to great success later in the week. Already the final scene, delivered against a crescendo of chimes and knocking heartbeats, makes a tremendous effect.'

But several critics didn't rate highly Burton's performance, and partly blamed it on us, his student fellow actors. Milton Shulman in the *Evening Standard* reported:

> Burton gives a restrained, measured, melodically spoken performance that only explodes into its true tragic and spiritual dimensions in Faustus's final speech in which he repents his bargain and faces the terrifying prospect of eternal damnation … But no actor can be great performing in a vacuum. And Burton had little success trying to get dramatic sparks flying when there was so much damp undergraduate tinder all around him.

Felix Barker in the *Evening News* wrote: 'Bearded, as the scholar-hero, he seemed to be holding his punches so as not to wipe the floor with the undergraduate amateurs with whom he was giving this exhibition bout.' Herbert Kretzmer in the *Daily Express*, under the headline 'So nice of the Burtons but...' wrote: 'From first to last, Mr Burton remains resolutely on his own, an eagle among a covey of well-meaning sparrows.' Alan Brien, in the *Sunday Telegraph*, decided to offer Burton an acting lesson:

> *Even the pleasure of hearing the famous anthology passages spoken with classic eloquence was finally denied us. Long ago, I compared Mr Burton's Old Vic delivery to that of the man in the I-Speak-Your-Weight machine, too perfectly modulated to be real. Now that effortless flow has been interrupted by his new habit of pausing in the middle of almost every phrase as though dictating to a secretary whose shorthand was rusty.*

The critics' treatment of Elizabeth Taylor was kinder, though occasionally peppered with facetious humour. Milton Shulman (*Evening Standard*) wrote: 'Miss Elizabeth Taylor ... glided majestically and serenely through her speech-less role.' Felix Barker (*Evening News*) wrote:

> *In golden white, and with diamante on her eyelids, Elizabeth Taylor made her entrance as Helen of Troy at the very end on a cloud of property smoke and through a trap door. The part gives her not a word to say, but oh yes, she looked as though she could easily launch a thousand ships. Faustus rightly took her off to bed and then, in a strangled last minute burst of passion, beseeched the ever-moving spheres of heaven to stand still.*

Herbert Kretzmer (*Daily Express*) said:

Elizabeth Taylor occurs twice in this solemn charade, very late in the evening. First she appears ankle deep in stage smoke. Next, she comes up from the basement on a hydraulic lift. She says nothing, but looks lovely on both occasions.

B.A. Young (*Financial Times*) said: 'Elizabeth Taylor makes quite a memorable moment of her wordless part, drifting onto the stage in a cloud of ectoplasm, and giving herself to Faustus like a passionate zombie.' Alan Brien (*Sunday Telegraph*) remained cynical:

If Mr Burton seemed to be determined to being typed as his screen image, Elizabeth Taylor looking impossibly pretty in a filmy nightie, on a carpet of smoke, was every boy's dream of a film star. But this was a Hollywood, or rather a television commercial version of Helen like a cunning soft-sell for lingerie.

W.A. Darlington (*Daily Telegraph*) wrote:

No actress better equipped with looks, charm and personality (not to speak of widespread fame) than Miss Taylor has ever been available or willing to fill out the part and give it dramatic significance. Her task was then comparatively easy. Mr Burton's, on the other hand, was of a difficulty made more daunting by Nevill Coghill's sombre and unhandy production, in which it did not seem that anything passionate or wicked was going on.

This criticism of Coghill's production was echoed by some, but not all, of the critics. Philip Hope-Wallace (the *Guardian*) wrote:

Nevill Coghill's production is full, elaborate and even a little self-indulgent in making as much as possible of the rather feeble conjuring tricks with which the author fills the middle of his play.

Felix Barker (*Evening News*) flattered with faint praise: 'I think Professor Nevill Coghill, the sensitive producer, had genuinely tried to take the heat out of an inflammable occasion with a scholarly interpretation. So, I feel rather cynical and Philistine for saying that I found this slap-up production of Marlowe's *Dr Faustus* under-lit, under-spoken, over-organed, and rather tedious.' Bernard Levin (*Daily Mail*) wrote, 'the director has not even had the sense to cut the abysmal clown scenes.' Herbert Kretzmer (*Daily Express*) criticised the production as 'a low-voltage evening in the theatre'. The *Stage* was kinder:

> *Professor Coghill, unlike so many dons, is an artist as well as a scholar, a man of the theatre with a musical ear for the aural splendours of Marlowe's finer language and a keen visual appreciation of effective staging which is not only visually appealing but, also, theatrically effective.*

The *Stage* critic was one of the very few kind enough to mention some of us undergraduates! 'Of the OUDS cast, Robert Scott, as the very well-spoken Chorus, Andreas Teuber, effectively chill and not unmoving, if a little too restrained, as Mephistophilis, David Wood as Wagner, and Ian Marter as the Duke of Vanholt are specially notable.'

Felix Barker (*Evening News*) continued his somewhat snide rant: 'Vast applause. Endless curtain calls. Professor Coghill (who had done a fine job by OUDS standards) extricated from the centre of a row, kissed Miss Taylor and whimsically thanked his stars. A curious night.' To pay tribute to the remarkable Coghill, without whom this unique event would not have happened, Harold Hobson (*Sunday Times*) not only praised him, but remembered landmark moments in his directing career. He wrote:

> *This production is a fitting reward to the abnegation of Miss Taylor and Mr Burton as well as a moving climax to the career of Professor*

*Coghill who has brought so great value to the often separated worlds
of learning and of the theatre ... Professor Coghill has a slick hand
with sensational entries. How he once made Ariel walk on the water
is still a legend far beyond the lake of Worcester and the tower of
Merton. In* A Midsummer Night's Dream *he breathtakingly brought
on Peggy Ashcroft and John Gielgud dancing to the footlights hand
in hand, clothed in absolute magic. Here the first entry of Lucifer
and Beelzebub, played by David McIntosh and Jeremy Eccles, is
similarly exciting. They are suddenly seen high up at the back of
the stage, emerging luridly out of darkness, enskied perhaps, but far
from sainted. Equally startling is the eruption of Andreas Teuber's
imaginatively melancholy and ambiguous Mephistophilis behind
the illustrious shoulder of Richard Burton.*

The reviews were never going to harm the box office – tickets had
quickly sold out, even though they cost from £1-10s. to £5-5s,
compared with the normal Saturday-night Playhouse maximum
of 12s for professional productions and 6s-6d for university
productions. A few cheaper unreserved tickets were available
only on the day of performance. And I cannot remember if any
of us showed any particular interest in the reviews or concern
about the less kind ones. Certainly all I remember from the week
of performances was that we lived in a fantasy world, where
everything revolved around the play.

Towards the end of the week, we students invited the Burtons
to a celebratory meal after the show. We took them to the Cantina,
a restaurant in Queen Street, near Carfax, not far from the theatre.
It was a happy occasion, with little formality. The Burtons had
become our friends. Towards the end of the evening, Sheila,
unbeknown to me, didn't feel well. Suddenly I felt a tap on the
shoulder and turned to see an anxious Elizabeth. 'Sheila's puking
in the john,' she told me. 'I've cleaned her up.' The upshot was that
Sheila and I were bundled into the Rolls, and driven by Gaston

back to my digs in Little Clarendon Street, while Richard and Elizabeth walked back to the Randolph. A typically kind gesture.

Their generosity continued. After the final Saturday-night performance, they threw a lavish party for us all. Back in the Randolph ballroom, where we had performed the run-through for them less than three weeks earlier, they entertained the cast and backstage team with free-flowing food and drink. Wood, Scott and Gould had been asked to provide the cabaret. We sang a selection of our comedy songs, which seemed to go down well. Richard and Elizabeth said nice things, then listened as we told them we were preparing a new musical revue to tour and play the Edinburgh Festival, after taking our final exams in early summer. We told them that the three of us would be joined by Adele Weston, with whom we had worked in *Hang Down Your Head and Die* and the musical *You Can't Do Much Without a Screwdriver*. Adele had a fine singing voice. Somehow, possibly led by the persuasive Bob, we found ourselves asking if the Burtons would become our patrons. Not only did they agree, but they offered to give us £250, a tidy sum, to put towards our running costs. It wasn't long before we had new letterhead paper, with the words 'WSG Productions, Patrons: Richard Burton and Elizabeth Taylor' proudly emblazoned at the top.

Well after midnight, realising that the dream was coming to its conclusion, everyone said their fond farewells. Sheila and I approached Elizabeth. 'See you tomorrow,' she smiled. At first we didn't understand, but then realised she was talking about the planned recording taking place next day. HMV, the famous EMI Records label, had asked to make an LP record of the production. We explained to Elizabeth that we had not been called for the next day's session in London. Sheila did not have a speaking role, and my few lines as Wagner were to be recorded at a later date. 'But you must come!' exclaimed Elizabeth. 'See you there!'

As we walked back to Little Clarendon Street, Sheila and I, convinced that Elizabeth's command had been sincere, decided that somehow we should make the trip to London. The next morning, having borrowed enough money for our train fares, we set off for Oxford railway station. This necessitated walking past my college, Worcester. For some reason it occurred to me to pop into the Porter's Lodge to see if there was any post in my pigeonhole. Bearing in mind it was Sunday, this was an odd thing to do. To my surprise I found a note. It was from Morgan, the Burtons' assistant agent. It asked me to urgently ring him at a number that turned out to be the Randolph Hotel. Checking I had the right coins, I hurried to the college phone box and dialled the number. 'Thank heaven I've found you!' exclaimed Morgan. He said that Elizabeth had given him instructions to contact Sheila and myself and offer to drive us to London. She had been most insistent, Morgan said. Not wanting to incur her displeasure, he had delayed his drive to town, determined to locate us. Sheila and I walked the short distance up Beaumont Street to the Randolph, where Morgan was waiting, with a very impressive Jaguar. As he raised the boot to drop in our modest luggage, we noticed it was lined with a deep pile of unopened Burtons' fan mail.

Soon we were enjoying a smooth and comfortable ride to Hampstead, where we were warmly welcomed by Richard and Elizabeth and his brother Ivor and the lovely Gwen, in their cosy house in Squire's Mount, just off Hampstead Heath. The six of us enjoyed lunch and a relaxing chat before it was time to set off for the recording studio in Putney. It was in the home of the independent producer, Denis Comper. Gaston drove Richard, Elizabeth, Sheila and myself in the Rolls. We rang the doorbell. Comper and his wife were staggered to find Elizabeth Taylor on their doorstep. Burton was expected, yes, but Elizabeth's non-speaking role in the play meant they had never dreamed of her attending. 'I'm here to make the sandwiches,' announced Elizabeth. And she did. For several hours she entertained us in the improvised green room upstairs, while Richard and some of the student cast recorded excerpts from the play. There were rumours of a row downstairs, when Kenneth

Allsop appeared uninvited and managed to insult Richard, who had him thrown out. I was blissfully unaware of this upstairs, enjoying Elizabeth regaling us with stories of Hollywood. And washing up. She seemed to enjoy doing 'normal' things. The climax came for me at midnight. The next day was my twenty-second birthday. As midnight struck, Elizabeth Taylor wished me many happy returns and kissed me on the lips. I glowed with pleasure, and still glow at the memory of this spontaneous gesture of affection. It wasn't a sensual kiss, rather a warm and sincere acknowledgement of the friendly and warm relationship I, Sheila and my fellow student actors had enjoyed with this very special lady and her very special husband. It marked the culmination of a magical, unique and truly unforgettable time.

A few days later I received a package containing a copy of Richard's book, *A Christmas Story*. It was signed, with birthday greetings from him and Elizabeth. My thoughtful stepfather, John Whittle, had managed to organise this unique gift, which I still treasure.

Thereafter, back to reality. The Burtons flew off to film *The Taming of the Shrew*. We students woke up from our brief admission to a dream world of celebrity. I tried to do a modest amount of work towards my finals a couple of months later. Sheila, however, managed to hit the newspaper headlines a fortnight after *Faustus* finished. Not for the happiest reasons. 'Liz's understudy sacked from Oxford,' announced the *Daily Mail*. The *Daily Mirror* reported:

Sheila, 19, must quit Oxford's Ruskin School of Drawing after completing only two years of her three-year painting course. She said in Oxford last night that she had missed some tutorials – 'one of which I forgot to go to, when the play Dr Faustus *was presented at the Oxford Playhouse.' Sheila, of Kingston, Surrey, added: 'The principal called me in and asked why I hadn't apologised to my tutors. There was a clash of personalities and the principal said he*

would prefer my absence to my presence. He said he would like me
to leave at the end of the summer term.'

The *Daily Sketch* carried a picture of Sheila and me standing either side of a smoking Burton. Quite how much this setback affected Sheila's later life we will never know, but by the end of the year we had married, and she had become a professional actress. Equity, the actors' union, already had a Sheila Dawson on their books, so Sheila had to change her surname. In a gesture of revenge against her college, she chose the name 'Ruskin'.

I suppose it was inevitable that, following the mixed critical reaction to Coghill's unique production, *Cherwell*, the university newspaper, should feel at liberty to ask on their front page – while the play was still running – 'WHAT MADE *DR FAUSTUS* FLOP?' The reporter invited comment on the unflattering notices. "'What do you expect from a pig but a grunt?" commented Professor Coghill yesterday. "I never read reviews anyway – they only depress me."' Bob, as OUDS President, was quoted as saying, 'The reviewers only cut up this show because they knew they had no control over its success at all.' My own reaction to the reviews was apparently, 'I was very disappointed – I admit there are some bad scenes, but they come from the writing of the play. The audience was largely to blame – they seemed so overawed by the occasion that they couldn't just sit back and laugh.' I'd like to think these words were put into my mouth. They make me sound disloyal.

Don Chapman, the *Oxford Mail* critic, put things in perspective with an article entitled 'Now that all the fuss has died down...'. He was surprised at the negative and somewhat cynical national newspaper reviews:

Personally, I hoped that the reviewers of the Sunday papers
would redress the balance. But no. Yesterday only Harold Hobson
enthused. And so it seems likely that rumour will add another

gaudy chapter to the already colourful legend that surrounds the visiting stars. But did Richard Burton and Elizabeth Taylor really waste their time coming to Oxford to appear with a nondescript bunch of students under the direction of an elderly professor on the brink of retirement? Of course not. Apart from the financial fact that their presence here has made possible the building of a theatre workshop by the university in the very near future, they brought to the production an artistic stature it could not have had otherwise, and Miss Taylor's contribution was unique.

I would like to think that Don's assessment that the production was more than a novelty was correct. Certainly, more than fifty years later, the production is remembered as arguably the most celebrated in the history of the Oxford Playhouse, and photos of the Burtons in character still grace the staircase walls. As Chapman summed up in his article:

So both these great stars can leave Oxford with their reputations unscarred, their standing as warm-hearted, generous, unpretentious personalities, enhanced, and their image – at least in the eyes of those who worked with them, met them, or saw them on the stage – given a new lustre. But it would be a pity if their visit is regarded simply as a freak of the friendship which exists between them and Prof. Coghill.

The LP record was released in June. 'Magnificent', praised one specialist magazine. Several students were a little disappointed that their contributions had been cut from the final product, but the recording was rightly a celebration of Burton's acting and beautiful voice. As such, it is an evocative reminder of the stage production, albeit only aural. No visual recording was made. However, as Burton had intimated in the press conference, the idea of making a film version of the production was discussed and eventually came to fruition. Many of the original cast joined the Burtons in Rome during the summer vacation. Bob and I were by then heavily involved in rehearsal and performance of our revue, *Four Degrees Over*. So we had to forego the film experience. Sheila took part and, by all accounts, good fun was had by all. Together, we attended a glittering premiere at the ABC cinema, Oxford, on 15 October, 1967, by which time we had been married for nearly a year. The Burtons came, and hosted a supper party afterwards, back at the Randolph Hotel. Critical reaction to the film was not enthusiastic but its aim of raising more money for the workshop fund was applauded.

So how much money was eventually raised? And what is the legacy of the *Dr Faustus* production? For a long time there was uncertainty, and no sign of a workshop being built. However, eventually, the Burton Rooms were built next door to the Playhouse. They were originally used as rehearsal rooms and the occasional performance. In the late 1980s, while Oxford Playhouse was closed, members of OUDS and other university drama groups started putting on plays in the venue, giving it the name the Burton Taylor Theatre. These days it is called the Burton Taylor Studio and is managed by Oxford Playhouse on behalf of the University of Oxford.

I never quite understood the detail of how the Burton Rooms had been funded. But in 2006, the Playhouse invited me to host an event at the Playhouse about the *Dr Faustus* experience, appearing onstage at the Playhouse with others involved, including Bob, Sheila and Andreas, who had flown from America for the occasion. Don Chapman, who, following his retirement from writing theatre reviews for the *Oxford Mail*, had written a definitive history of Oxford Playhouse, sent an e-mail contribution to Tish Francis, co-director of the theatre at the time, telling the rather sad story of what happened:

Dr Faustus ran a week and made a profit of about £12,000 towards the Workshop Fund. When Burton decided to make a film of it, Coghill boasted that it would make about £125,000. So the University Theatre Curators decided they could go for a more grandiose development. In fact the film, released on the back of the Burton-Taylor hit The Taming of the Shrew, *was a disaster and didn't even recover its costs. 'No problem,' said Burton, he would bankroll it out of his own pocket. The trouble was he didn't have the cash. His Hollywood attorney, Aaron Frosch, controlled the purse strings and getting money out of him was like squeezing blood out of a stone. It took ten years and by then inflation had halved the value. That and the curators' ineptitude resulted in a building, which as Barry Sheppard (the former Playhouse administrator) rightly said had more corridor and staircase space than performance space. Even so, it was used by some iconic fringe groups like Hull-Truck and Gay Sweatshop. Gyles Brandreth put stuff on there during his two summer festivals and the* Observer *bankrolled a couple of student-inspired spring festivals. Meanwhile, Roy Copeman, the director of Oxford Youth Theatre, got the City Council to build the 200-seater Pegasus Theatre in Magdalen Road for £30,000! The best performance space in Oxford.*

In my *Dr Faustus* scrapbook is a poster advertising a celebratory ball on Thursday 24 February 1966, in the Randolph Hotel ballroom. This event, a few days after our final performance, has totally escaped my memory, even though, as OUDS Steward, I would have been one of the organisers. I'm beginning to believe it never took place, but perhaps another *Dr Faustus* veteran might put me right.

But my memory remains clear about Richard's fiftieth birthday party that night at the Dorchester in 1975, which occurred only weeks after the Burtons had famously remarried – they had divorced in 1974 – and would divorce again in 1976. And fate had decreed that Sheila and I, too, had divorced, in 1973. By the time of Richard's birthday bash, Jacqueline Stanbury and I had been married for nearly a year. Richard Burton died, aged fifty-eight, in 1984. Elizabeth Taylor became a Dame in 2000, and she died, aged seventy-nine, in 2011.

Over fifty years later, I'm still lucky enough to visit Oxford regularly, when my children's plays are touring to the Playhouse or the New Theatre, and in my role as Trustee of the splendid institution The Story Museum. Every time I pass the Burton Taylor Studio, the Playhouse itself and the Randolph Hotel next door, my mind journeys back to 1966 and the magical days ... when Hollywood came to Oxford.

Fifty-Five Years On...

This is what happened to some of the principal players in the *Dr Faustus* production.

Professor Nevill Coghill died, aged eighty-one, in 1980. Soon after directing *Dr Faustus*, he retired as Merton Professor of English Literature. In 1968, the musical version of *Canterbury Tales* that he co-wrote, based on his translation, enjoyed great success in London's West End and on Broadway.

Robert Scott (OUDS President, Chorus/Faustus understudy) became a successful theatre administrator, notably in Manchester. He was Chairman of the Manchester Olympic Bid Committee's unsuccessful bids in 1996 and 2000, as well as the successful November 1995 bid to play host to the 2002 Commonwealth Games. Sir Bob was knighted in 1994.

Andreas Teuber (Mephistophilis) was Associate Professor of Philosophy at Brandeis University in the United States. He died in 2021.

Sheila Dawson (Dancer/Helen of Troy understudy) and I married in 1966 and divorced in 1973. Having changed her surname, Sheila Ruskin has had a successful acting career.

Richard Durden-Smith (Evil Angel, Mephistophilis understudy) and **Maria Aitken** (Good Angel) were married but later divorced. Both have had successful careers as professional actors. Richard dropped the Smith to become Richard Durden. Maria has also directed, notably the theatre production of *The 39 Steps*.

Richard Carwardine (Valdez) was President of Corpus Christi College, Oxford, from 2010–2016. He is a Pro-Vice Chancellor of the university. A historian, best known for his work on Abraham Lincoln.

Richard Heffer (1st Scholar), **Nicholas Loukes** (The Cardinal, died 1976), **Ian Marter** (The Emperor, died 1986) and **Bruce Alexander** (Vintner) all became professional actors.

Hugh Williams (2nd Scholar) became a highly experienced media executive, with a long history of senior roles at the BBC. He also wrote the bestselling history book, *50 Things You Need to Know About British History*.

Gwydion Thomas (3rd Scholar) spent a lifetime in higher education, teaching English, Art and Design. He died in 2016.

David McIntosh (Lucifer) and **Antony Braime** (Envy) became successful businessmen. Antony Braime died in 2006.

Jeremy Eccles (Beelzebub) has lived in Australia since 1982. He writes and broadcasts about the performing arts, particularly opera. Much of his writing (and the occasional film) is about Aboriginal art.

Nicholas Gray (Pride) became, as Nick Gray, a television documentary producer/director. He was Visiting Professor of Documentary Production, University of Lincoln.

Phillip Hodson (Covetousness) became a psychotherapist, broadcaster and author, who specialised in 'phone-in' therapy in his role as Britain's first 'agony uncle'.

Alan Moses (Gluttony) is a former Lord Justice of Appeal, a Court of Appeal Judge. Sir Alan became Chairman of the Independent Press Standards Organisation.

Patrick Barwise (Sloth), emeritus Professor of Management and Marketing at London Business School, has published widely on management, marketing and media.

Jenny Moss (Lechery) was for a time an actress and model. As Natasha Morgan she then became a counsellor and psychotherapist.

David Jessel (a Knight) became a well-known TV and radio news presenter, author and campaigner against miscarriages of justice. From 2000–2010 he was also a commissioner of the Criminal Cases Review Commission.

Sebastian Walker (a Horse-courser) founded in 1979, the highly successful Walker Books, one of the first companies to publish exclusively children's books. He died in 1991, aged forty-nine.

Richard Alford (Duke of Vanholt) was Director of the British Council in Italy from 1996–2003. He was made a Companion of the Order of St Michael and St George (CMG) in the Queen's Birthday Honours list, 2003.

Nicholas Young (Assistant Director) has for many years been the Artistic Director of Rainbow Theatre, specialising in theatre for young people, including Shakespeare productions.

Jane Wilford (Stage Manager) had two distinct careers, first as a journalist working mostly in Africa and later as a successful doctor specialising in occupational health. She died in 2013, aged sixty-seven.

Andrew Hilton (Robin) had a long career in economics and international finance, eventually as Director (and co-founder) of the Centre for the Study of Financial Innovation.

Susan Watson (Demon Wife), in her married name, Sue Griffin, was the National Training Manager for the National Childminding Association. She contributed to the initial development of NVQs, and has written books and articles. She became a Justice of the Peace.

Roger Sherman (Old Man) became a major player in the world of trade fairs.

Jacqueline Harvey (Choreographer/Dancer), as Jackie Kiers, worked professionally as a Director/Choreographer and teacher of physical theatre. She now undertakes theatre criticism.

Sheila Peskett (Dancer), whose name was wrongly spelled in the programme, became a Consultant in Rheumatology and Rehabilitation Medicine.

Geoffrey Nice (Friar) was appointed Queen's Counsel in 1990. Sir Geoffrey became Vice Chair of the Bar Standards Board, and Professor of Law at Gresham College. He has been involved with the International Criminal Tribunal for the Former Yugoslavia, and was Deputy Prosecutor at the trial of Slobodan Milošević.

Petronella Pulsford (Lady-in-Waiting) acted professionally as Petronella Ford, and wrote the novel *Lee's Ghost*.

Hazel Neary (Dancer), as Hazel Anderson, became an archivist in London and Scotland, and also a long-standing volunteer for Deaf Direct.

Peter Wiles (Production Manager) worked professionally in the theatre and became a freelance professional photographer.

Apologies to the *Faustus* alumni whose subsequent history I have been unable to uncover.

WINTER WITH MISS WINTERS

1972

The Vamp starring Shelley Winters

Out of the blue, the opportunity to star opposite Hollywood legend Shelley Winters. What an adventure! What an experience...

A few days before Christmas 1971, I found myself at a loose end in London and just for fun decided to visit Harrods Food Hall. Visiting Harrods wasn't something I did regularly, but I always enjoyed looking at the impressive fresh food counters, overflowing with fruit from all over the world, as well as fish of every size and shape. I never bought anything, but enjoyed having a look. Things had slowed down a bit. I had opened *The Owl and the Pussycat Went to See...* in its glamorous West End location, the Apollo Theatre, and another of my children's plays, *The Plotters of Cabbage Patch Corner*, directed by Jonathan Lynn, at the Shaw Theatre, its first ever Christmas production. A new play was in rehearsal at the Swan Theatre, Worcester, where all my early efforts began. *Flibberty and the Penguin* was due to open on Boxing Day. Acting-wise, there was nothing on the horizon.

As I left Harrods, a sprig of heather was suddenly thrust into my face by a woman I assumed was a gypsy. She insisted that the heather would give me good luck. Quite why I didn't take no notice and just move on, I don't know. That would probably have been my usual reaction. But I found myself searching in my pocket for a couple of coins, handing them over and receiving the heather, not believing that good luck would come from the gesture, but rather smugly feeling I had done a good deed. Then I went home to my flat in North Cheam, a bus ride from the end of the Northern line.

As I opened the front door, I heard the phone ringing. It was John Miller, my agent. I was a bit surprised, because it was after

51

6pm and therefore after office hours. But John said he had been determined to reach me, because London Weekend Television wanted me to go along for an interview for a play. They wanted me to go immediately. Again, this seemed odd, because auditions were never in the early evening. But I said yes, of course, and jumped in the car.

Paul Knight, the producer, and John Reardon, the director, welcomed me and explained that they were doing a play for television called *The Vamp*, which was a two-hander. They were interested in me playing one of the two roles, Colin, a young film buff, who, walking along Park Lane one day, sees a woman he is convinced is a famous film star, a Greta Garbo type somewhat past her prime, who these days is rarely seen in public. The young man follows her, sees where she lives, buys her a bunch of flowers and boldly rings her doorbell. She lets him in, he gushes with compliments, she is flattered, talks about herself and ends up trying to seduce him, before sadly realising that her heyday is past. I expressed interest in playing the part, of course, and was intrigued to learn that the play had been written by John Kane, a splendid actor whom I had last seen playing Puck in the celebrated Royal Shakespeare Company production of *A Midsummer Night's Dream* in 1970, directed by Peter Brook.

At this point in the interview, Paul told me that the faded film star was to be played by Shelley Winters, who would be coming from America to play the role. Although I was not a film buff like the character they had described, I did know that Shelley Winters had won two Oscars, for *The Diary of Anne Frank* in 1959 and for *A Patch of Blue* in 1965. And I remembered that she had been in a famous film called *A Place in the Sun* (1951). Not to mention Stanley Kubrick's *Lolita* (1962) and Lewis Gilbert's *Alfie* (1966), with Michael Caine. I also knew she was a respected stage actress, who had acted many times on Broadway, notably in *The Night of the Iguana* in 1961. I was also pretty sure that she had studied the

Method style of acting, taught at the Actors' Studio by Lee Strasberg. My only previous experience of working with a Method actress had been in David Mercer's *After Haggerty*, for the Royal Shakespeare Company in 1970. Billie Dixon came from America to play opposite Frank Finlay. She was very good, but not very consistent. The Method tended, I thought, to create selfish actors, who could only think of their own character and situation, with little empathy with any other character onstage. At the dress rehearsal of *After Haggerty*, Frank Finlay had come onstage to have a scene with Billie, and couldn't find her. She was hiding behind the door. He made a joke of it, looking for her under the desk, behind the curtain or in a cupboard, but Billie's action destroyed the flow of the play. When asked about her behaviour by the director, she explained that she just didn't feel quite like talking to Frank at that moment, which seemed a strange thing to say when you are acting in a play!

Naturally I was very excited by the prospect of working with Miss Winters, and said so. To my amazement, they then offered me the part, without asking me to read or audition in any way. I said yes. They said they would talk to my agent. I walked back to the car in darkness, suddenly remembering the sprig of heather that was still in my pocket...

Rehearsals started soon after Christmas, on 17 January, 1972. They took place in a very large room several floors up in Station House, home of London Weekend's offices, in Neasden, just off the North Circular. On the first morning Miss Winters arrived late, having been driven in a limousine. She was friendly, slightly nervous, I felt, and plumper than I had expected. She was fifty-one. I was nearly twenty-eight. John, the director, took us through a reading of the play. He was a gentle man, who diplomatically didn't offer too much direction, and accepted a few rewrite ideas from Miss Winters.

Over the next few days, we blocked the play, although it was clear that Miss Winters wasn't used to being tied down to definite moves too soon. She wanted the freedom to let her performance grow organically. This was fine in principle, but made it difficult for John to create his camera script. Also, most mornings, Miss Winters, or Shelley as I was now able to call her, would announce with relish, 'Fresh cuts'. This meant that we all had to sit down and go through the whole script, with her suggesting changes. She was fairly insistent that these rewrites were necessary, and John went along with most of them. But then she suggested that a new script should be typed up, to make things clearer. So several times, overnight, a new script was prepared, only to be changed again the next morning.

Shelley was always kind to me. After a week or so it became apparent that she had difficulty learning the lines, of which there were a lot. She started calling me her 'rock'. This meant that I had to keep maximum concentration, so that I never gave her the wrong cue. Once or twice, when I messed up, she crowed, in a sing-song voice, 'David's made a mista-ake!'

During the coffee break, on the first or second day of rehearsal, Shelley produced a polythene bag, from which she tipped onto the tabletop a large number of pills, of different sizes and colours. Picking out a few, she said, with humour, 'I'll have one of those, one of those, two of those, and that's for my thyroid....' The handful of pills was swiftly swallowed, and before long Shelley was yawning. She would announce that she needed a rest, and from lunchtime till about 5pm, she would have a lie down. This was made possible by the fact that the rehearsal room had been divided by screens into two halves. On one side the set of the play was, as usual, marked out on the floor, with poles suggesting door frames. In the other half was a fully furnished luxury hotel room, complete with dressing table and double bed. Shelley would retire and the production team and I would have to stay quiet. After a couple of days of this, John offered me the use of a small office along the corridor, from which I was told I could make phone calls to anywhere in the world! Then, when Shelley woke up, we would resume rehearsal, which would carry on into the evening.

As we progressed, the scenes in which Miss Bennett tried to seduce Colin became increasingly improvised and uninhibited. Shelley would push me onto the sofa and lie on top of me. This was often quite funny and good-natured. But then she took to trying to rip open my shirt. Several times buttons popped off and buttonholes were torn. Two or three shirts were damaged, and London Weekend kindly paid me for replacements.

It was wintertime. Shelley began complaining about the cold. She was staying with the film critic and columnist Peter Noble and his wife, who were old friends. But she found their house in St John's Wood so chilly that she transferred to a room in the Royal Lancaster Hotel. She asked, during the run-up to the studio days, if we could help her by running the lines. So, in the evening, John, plus a stage manager and myself, would sweat profusely in Shelley's hotel room, going through the play with her. She was tucked up in bed wearing a tracksuit and a thick sweater and a woollen hat. We wore T-shirts and were still boiling.

Unfortunately, by the time we started work in the studio, Shelley was still not quite on top of the lines. And this made her nervous. When recording started it became clear that we would have to do the play section by section. Some were necessarily quite long, so demanded retake after retake, which Shelley was very reluctant to do. I was very grateful for the fact that she never showed me the rough side of her tongue, but the long-suffering floor manager, as well as the producer and director, were shouted at quite often. Furthermore, for much of the play, in order to make herself look younger, she insisted on having tapes attached to her face, stretching the skin, then tied tightly under her wig. This was painful, and could only remain like that for a few minutes before she had to release the tapes and have a rest. In each break, she tried to relax her mind by listening to opera on her portable cassette player. She didn't have earphones, so the music would play loudly in the studio, until she announced she was ready to continue.

There were lighter moments. Early on, Shelley enjoyed entertaining the crew during the necessary pauses in recording. She sang 'Life Upon the Wicked Stage' from *Showboat*, and, revealing her left-wing credentials, regaled us with what now might be regarded as a politically incorrect song about appeasement: 'Toodle-ama-ama, Toodle-ama-ama Appeasement today, Toodle-ama-ama, Toodle-ama-ama Nations we give away … We're opposed you see, To any real democracy … We flew off to Munich, gave all to that eunuch…'

Shelley was witty. As I lay with my head on her shoulder, the floor manager mentioned a 'two-shot'. Quick as a flash, Shelley cried, 'Two-shot – one bosom and him?'

The sound engineers, rather naughtily, decided to record her off-camera remarks and tirades. They presented me with a cassette copy at the end of recording. They revealed her occasional volatility, but, perhaps more significantly, her insecurity. Her frustration was, of course, echoed by the producer, the director and the floor manager, who all bent over backwards to be patient and reassuring, despite their concerns. After a highly dramatic scene, in which Shelley chased me around and along a sofa, shouting and sometimes hitting me, she collapsed, exhausted. John, the director, came down. She knew what was coming…

SHELLEY:	*You don't want me to do that again? Don't tell me that.*
JOHN:	*I would love to do it just once more.*
SHELLEY:	*Oh honey.*
JOHN:	*Just once more. Once more.*
SHELLEY:	*I don't think I'll be able to go through the day. Okay I'll try. What did we do wrong?*
JOHN:	*Just some little things on the lines.*
SHELLEY:	*I thought the lines were perfect.*

She would suddenly want to change the blocking or the tempo:

SHELLEY: *Can we move across somewhere? Is that*
            what's fucking up? I can go slower. You
            want me to go slower? I want to go slower.
            Okay?

One day my mother and stepfather were allowed to come to the studio and sit in the viewing gallery. Then they were invited to have lunch with me and Shelley. This was a kind gesture, but turned into quite an event, with a three-course meal. It lasted much longer than was, in the circumstances, advisable.

After lunch, Shelley started a scene and forgot her lines. She shook her head and sighed:

SHELLEY: *I don't know what I say and I don't know how to*
            fix my brain so I'll know. I'm just exhausted and
            was stupid to sit at lunch and socialise, have a
            big meal and wait for steaks to come up and it's
            insanity. This is the most demanding role I've ever
            done and I can't do it like this and I'm crazy. I don't
            know what the fuck to do.

The floor manager softly gave her her line.

SHELLEY: *That doesn't do any good honey. I don't do parts*
            by lines. That's why this is driving me crazy. I don't
            act that way with words. I act with ideas. And I'm
            just saying words. The performance today is just
            words. And I just don't know what to do.

The floor manager tried to reassure her, but to no avail.

SHELLEY: *I'm going from word to word instead of ideas and*
            I'm, I'm, er, getting very panicky. And I can't have

> *the production manager banging on my door when*
> *my stockings have run and saying how long is it*
> *going to be. You know I'm trying to go fast and it*
> *just makes me more nervous.*

Paul, the producer came down to the floor and told her things were going well.

SHELLEY: *Well, honey, I'm telling you I can't work under this*
            kind of pressure. I'm an actress who doesn't work
            with words. I work with ideas. Now – my stocking's
            developed a run, the girl ran to get some new ones.
            He's knocking on the door saying how long is it
            going to be? What am I doing? Fucking somebody?
            I'm going as fast as I can. It puts me under terrible
            pressure. It's a part with endless speeches in this
            thing and if I start going like this you're going to be
            here for three weeks!

PRODUCER: *No, we won't, we're getting on nicely—*

SHELLEY: *Well, you are. I'm not. I'm saying words, I'm not*
            acting, I'm saying words. I'm doing an empty
            performance. I know when I'm performing and I'm
            just saying words. I'm very disappointed with what
            I did up there and I don't want to do it here. And I
            don't know what to do about it. And I'm not going
            to be rushed or harassed.

PRODUCER: *[More confidence-boosting and suggesting that we*
            break for half an hour.]

SHELLEY: *No, I don't want half an hour. I want people to*
            leave me alone and let me act. Everybody can clear
            the stage too. I don't like people walking around in
            my eye-line.

Later on, the memory of lunch still haunted her:

> SHELLEY: *I'm so full of that eight course meal, sitting there waiting for … I mean, it was insanity. In America we eat a salad. I'm sitting down having starters and salad and meat and … waiting for steak and cheese and fruit, when I should be resting and thinking about what I'm doing…*

Colin, my character, called Shelley's character 'Miss Bennett'. Her first name was Barbara. The studio set comprised rooms in her apartment, furnished in a fairly lavish Hollywood style. On one wall, the size of a door, was a glamorous photo of the younger Miss Bennett, wearing what I think is called a basque, with fishnet tights. The black garment corseted the actress's middle, exaggerating the narrowness of her waist, to contrast with the curves of her hips and bust. At first glimpse I thought 'Marilyn Monroe'. Indeed there is a famous picture of Miss Monroe in this iconic pose. Shelley assured me that in fact this was an early promotional shot of herself, the pose for which was later poached by Miss Monroe and her publicists. She told me the two of them had once shared an apartment as budding starlets.

We recorded in story order. So the dramatic climax of the play was shot towards the end. My character suddenly flings open the curtains to allow natural light to flood in on Miss Bennett's face, rather sadly revealing the ravages of time. Shelley was really impressive in this scene, partly because she bravely insisted on removing the tapes that had so far lifted her face. She wore less make-up too. She recognised that this honesty was necessary to make the scene work. My character was cruelly calling her 'old', and she knew her face had to back up his comment.

The Vamp overran in the television studio by two days. Such an overrun was unheard of. The cost must have been considerable.

Two programmes had to be rescheduled. David Frost's weekly live programme was transferred to another location. An episode of *On the Buses* was apparently cancelled or postponed. But eventually our play was in the can and, with relief, London Weekend Television held a celebratory end-of-shoot party. Rex Firkin, the Executive Producer, took me to one side and thanked me for my patience and forbearance. I said it had been something of a rocky ride, but I was thrilled to have been part of it. He kindly said that my contribution would not be forgotten and that very soon I would be working for the company again. In fact it was to be many years before they employed me again!

Shelley stayed in London for a couple of days to do some promotion. I was invited to join her for a lunch interview at a posh restaurant called Odins. I remember Michael Parkinson was sitting at the next table. Jimmy Hill, the famous footballer, who had become a high-profile PR person for London Weekend, hosted the lunch, at which Weston Taylor, the *News of the World* reporter, was invited to ask questions. I kept quiet as Shelley regaled him with scandalous tales of how she had 'looked after' famous British actors when they first came to New York or Hollywood, including Sean Connery. In my naivety I was surprised by her indiscretions, but realised she was giving Mr Taylor a great story. I found myself feeling protective towards Shelley, wishing she wouldn't display such honesty.

Shelley asked me to accompany her to the theatre to see Ted Whitehead's play *Alpha Beta* at the Royal Court, starring Albert Finney and Rachel Roberts. We were chauffeur-driven to the theatre. Shelley wore a black coat and headscarf. She was unrecognisable. For me, it was rather like taking my auntie to the theatre. She told me that Albert Finney was another of the young actors she had 'looked after' when he came to America, and that he had invited us backstage to meet him after the play. In fact I already knew Albert, who was, along with Michael Medwin, one of the producers of Lindsay Anderson's film *If...*, in which I had played a rebel schoolboy alongside Malcolm McDowell three years earlier. The play was gritty and draining, but very well performed. Afterwards we found Albert's dressing room and were warmly received. Shortly afterwards there was a knock on the door, and a head appeared. A short gentleman with a familiar face greeted Albert, congratulating him on his performance. I suddenly realised it was Kirk Douglas. Behind him, not yet in the room, was a woman I assumed was his wife. Suddenly Mr Douglas saw Shelley. His demeanour changed. With a brief 'Hi Shelley!', he excused himself and almost pushed his wife back, as he departed, shutting the door behind him. I have always wondered exactly what this signified.

Before leaving London, Shelley gave me a photo of herself taken a couple of decades earlier. On it she wrote, 'For David. If I were this young and strong when we did *The Vamp* you would be coming back to the USA with me. Thank you, Darling, Shelley'.

It came as a surprise that I was paid overtime for the studio overrun. Even more of a surprise was that the amount was enough to take me for a few days' break in New York. In between the Broadway theatre trips and meetings to try to garner interest in my children's plays, I saw Shelley several times. We had a couple of meals together and she very kindly took me to the Lincoln Center Library, where they have an interesting theatre history section. She even bought me some beautiful reproductions of Edwardian London theatre posters. On another memorable day she took me to Lee Strasberg's Actors Studio, where we sat on a side balcony watching students performing solo pieces to Mr Strasberg. I think it was an end-of-term series of presentations, which would be evaluated with critical feedback. The actors appeared nervous. They had presumably worked hard building up to this exam. Mr Strasberg, their guru, was not one of their regular teachers, but as principal of the school, and creator of The Method, he had achieved legendary, god-like status.

One poor student made several false starts to his Hamlet speech, then gave up and walked offstage before judgement could be pronounced. Another student suffered with a trembling leg. While preparing to perform, standing centre-stage, he whispered to his leg, imploring it to stop wobbling. Eventually he gave up and sat down instead. He performed his speech. After a pause, Mr Strasberg wearily asked him how long he had been studying at the school. 'Three years,' came the reply. Mr Strasberg, a voice from the darkened auditorium, retorted: 'What a waste of our time, and yours.' The student, holding back tears, stumbled offstage.

Shelley didn't react during this cruel display. As a former Method student, I suppose she didn't feel such unsettling tuition was unusual. Maybe she credited her successful career to Mr Strasberg. She had certainly worked with some of his other students, including James Dean, Marlon Brando and Marilyn Monroe.

A few months later I was in Toronto, acting opposite Sir Michael Redgrave in John Mortimer's *A Voyage Round My Father*. On my way home I returned to New York for more theatre-going and meetings. Shelley invited me to visit her in her Central Park apartment. The date was fixed and she also offered to take me to the theatre that evening. She probably hadn't realised that the day chosen was Thanksgiving. When I arrived, there was a celebratory party going on. Shelley's welcoming maid ushered me in. I didn't know any of the guests, but Shelley, who was lying on a chaise longue, seemed happy to see me, although she was a little under the weather, having perhaps drunk quite a lot of celebratory alcohol. I was impressed to see her two Oscars gracing the mantlepiece, and happy to meet 'Tori', Shelley's daughter, who would have been about nine years younger than me. Her father was Vittorio Gassman, the Italian theatre and film actor and director, to whom Shelley had been married for a brief two years in the 1950s.

Shelley apologised for the fact that she felt unable to go to the theatre that night, but suggested I go with Tori. This I did, and we enjoyed Jason Miller's play *That Championship Season*, which won the Tony Award for Best Play in 1973.

By that time, *The Vamp* had been transmitted, on 1 October, 1972. It had originally been scheduled to be shown on 4 June. I never found out the reason for the delay. We got mixed reviews, which was to be expected, but on the whole Shelley's appearance in a British television play was welcomed and applauded. Leonard Buckley, reviewing the play in *The Times*, wrote that Miss Winters had grasped the opportunity to play the role of the 'time-worn actress' and had 'clasped it to her bosom'. He said that 'the effect was electric'. He was kind to me, too, and probably was correct when he said:

> She was joined by David Wood. He played a young English fan who came to pray, remained to scoff and nearly lost his virginity in between. His was a splendid performance, too. He did all that could have been asked of him. But what chance had he against Miss Winters? He spoke, but we looked at her.

I'm sorry that I never met this larger-than-life, warm-hearted, talented yet vulnerable lady again. In 1972 she came to prominence once more in *The Poseidon Adventure* and her other later films included *Pete's Dragon* (1977). She appeared on television in several episodes of *Roseanne*, and wrote three autobiographical books. She died in 2005, at the age of eighty-five, in Beverly Hills.

TOTTERING TOWERS

1975

Jeeves starring David Hemmings

A supporting role in a West End musical, based on the works of a classic comedy author, with book by Alan Ayckbourn and music by Andrew Lloyd Webber, starring a Hollywood leading man. What could possibly go wrong?

As I was lowered from the flies hanging upside down from a chandelier, the Gallery First Nighters shouted 'Rubbish!'. My indignation and embarrassment were tempered by the fact that I couldn't help agreeing with their criticism of what I had always considered an unnecessary and illogical moment of derring-do. It felt like the frustrating and inevitable culmination of an expensive, doomed theatrical endeavour. As David Hemmings extricated me from the branches of the chandelier and helped me stand upright while unclasping my safety harness, he shared with me a look of resigned sympathy. At least I was able to make a speedy exit. He had to carry on amidst a barrage of discontent from the gods.

The show was *Jeeves*, and this memorable first night was on 22 April, 1975. David played Bertie Wooster. I was Bingo Little. We were on the stage of the beautiful Her Majesty's Theatre in London's West End. Most of the newspaper critics agreed with the Gallery First Nighters and the musical limped to a demoralising conclusion a few short weeks later.

Jeeves was a spectacular flop, but I wouldn't have missed it for the world. Towards the end of our rollercoaster ride, David told me he was going to write a memoir called *Tottering Towers*. This play on words was a reference to Totleigh Towers, the main setting for the show. But in David's autobiography, *Blow-up and Other Exaggerations*, published in 2004, he dismisses *Jeeves* in just a few lines, remembering it as 'a mess' and 'a fiasco'. The memories

I recall here will give a flavour of what happened, from the point of view of a supporting actor.

By the time *Jeeves* was planned, David Hemmings had become a Hollywood star. He had come to prominence in 1966 in Antonioni's film *Blow-up*, which colourfully reflected London's Swinging Sixties scene. This led to his appearances in *Camelot* and *The Charge of the Light Brigade* and he also starred in *Barbarella* and *Alfred the Great*. It may have seemed surprising at first that he should play P.G. Wodehouse's Bertie Wooster in a musical. He hadn't appeared onstage for ten years. Yet he had been a notable boy soprano, featuring in English Opera Group performances of the works of Benjamin Britten. In later years he had recorded an album of songs.

David proved to be a much-loved leader of the *Jeeves* company. He was kind and approachable. I don't think any of us were aware of the fact that, as we began rehearsals, he was in the throes of a divorce from the actress Gayle Hunnicutt, and would later marry his secretary, Prudence, whom we regularly saw with him. David was the only actor I have ever worked with who could start drinking white wine in the middle of the morning, in rehearsal, and continue drinking until the end of the day without it appearing to have any adverse effect on his performing abilities. Unfortunately our director decided to join in, which perhaps occasionally clouded his judgement.

My first meeting with David was at Sydmonton, the country residence near Newbury of Andrew Lloyd Webber, our composer. I remember David genially trouncing me at the snooker table. We were guests at a pre-rehearsal party, when the prospects for *Jeeves* looked highly promising.

The pedigree of the creatives was impeccable. Andrew's huge West End successes with *Joseph and the Amazing Technicolor Dreamcoat* (1968) and *Jesus Christ Superstar* (1970) promised the possibility of another musical hit. Andrew was now to be working on his new musical without his lyricist Tim Rice, and this adaptation of the work of P.G. Wodehouse, arguably our greatest comic novelist, seemed an ideal task for Alan Ayckbourn, who was already highly regarded for his West End successes *Relatively Speaking* and *How the Other Half Loves*. I was fortunate enough to know both Andrew and Alan, and theirs seemed a perfect partnership for this project.

My first meeting with Andrew was at a welcome gathering for new members of the Experimental Theatre Club at Oxford University ten years earlier. Andrew had just arrived, having won a scholarship to Magdalen College to read History. He was seventeen years old, but with enviable confidence told me that his aim was to change the face of British musical theatre. I was in my second year and had already had a wonderful time, acting and singing in *Hang Down Your Head and Die*, the anti-capital punishment revue that had transferred to the West End, and directing a musical called *You Can't Do Much Without a Screwdriver*. Our mutual interest in musical theatre led to Andrew inviting me to play the title role in the musical *Dr Barnardo* (later retitled *The Likes of Us*) that he was writing with his friend Tim Rice. There was the possibility of a student production try-out at the Oxford Playhouse. Andrew invited me to his rooms, sat at the piano, and played and sang to me some of the catchiest songs I had ever heard. We chatted away without noticing the time, and suddenly realised that his college gates would be locked. He gamely helped me climb a precariously high wall until I dropped over the other side into Queens Lane and walked back to my college hostel. I never got to play Dr Barnardo, but always believed that Andrew's talent and dedication would produce great things.

In 1971 I met Alan Ayckbourn, having been cast in his play *Me Times Me Times Me*. We opened at the Phoenix Theatre, Leicester, before touring the UK on our way to the West End. Unfortunately we never made it to London. The play was brilliantly constructed, and the first two scenes were very funny, but the producers felt the final scene didn't live up to expectations, and our tour came to a close at the Theatre Royal, Bath. Some years later, under the title *Family Circles*, the play was successfully produced, but was never regarded as one of Ayckbourn's triumphs. In fact, when *Jeeves*, too, had failed to take off, Alan introduced me to a colleague as 'the man with the unlucky knees'. This was an amusing reference to the fact that in both productions I had worn tennis shorts.

Although I had never met him, I had huge respect and admiration for our director, Eric Thompson. At the time he was probably best known for his wonderfully wacky, off-the-wall writing and narrating of the animation series *The Magic Roundabout*. But he had notably directed Alan's West End productions of *Time and Time Again*, *The Norman Conquests* and *Absurd Person Singular*. And his production of R.C. Sherriff's masterpiece *Journey's End* for the 69 Theatre Company had completely bowled me over in the early '70s. I saw the production in three very different spaces, the University Theatre, Manchester, the Mermaid Theatre and the Cambridge Theatre in the West End. It was simply stunning.

So I was thrilled to be invited to audition for *Jeeves*. On the stage of the Palace Theatre, where *Jesus Christ Superstar* was still playing, I sang 'Gigi', the Lerner and Loewe song, which I had been asked to prepare. Anthony Bowles listened and didn't appear to disapprove. He was to be our musical director, having worked on *Jesus Christ Superstar* with sparkling effect. This eccentrically camp, sometimes wittily acerbic, musical genius was to prove a great ally to us all in rehearsal.

I was offered the role, and I obviously accepted straightaway. The script arrived and contained significantly more pages than a usual playscript. Its main inspiration was Wodehouse's *The Code of the Woosters*. Despite the fact that my character, Bingo Little, the eternal romantic, had little to do in the book, Alan had given him

TV TIMES
7, HIGH HOLBORN,
LONDON, W.C.1
ISSUE DATED 28 SEP 1972

SHELLEY WINTERS as Barbara Bennet in **THE VAMP** by JOHN KANE

with DAVID WOOD as Colin

Fading American film star Barbara Bennet is furious when her agent fails to get her a big part in a new movie.

There's obviously a conspiracy...

Then, a young man delivers flowers to her, and Barbara sees the opportunity of proving that the old appeal is still there.

Shelley Winters – looking for a man to dominate her: pages 14-16

MUSIC JOHN DANKWORTH : DESIGNER MARTIN JOHNSON : DIRECTOR JOHN REARDON : PRODUCER PAUL KNIGHT : EXECUTIVE PRODUCER REX FIRKIN *London Weekend Television Production*

tonight at 10.15

The Vamp: TV Times *listing.*

The Vamp: *The article in* Weekend *magazine.*

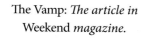

WEEKEND, April 5-11, 1972   21

In her forthcoming play for London Weekend television, *The Vamp*, Shelley plays an old vaudeville star visited by a young admirer

The Vamp: *Shelley Winters and me.*

THE TIMES
PRINTING HOUSE SQUARE,
LONDON, E.C.4.

ISSUE DATED   2 OCT 1972

Weekend TV

The Vamp
London Weekend

Leonard Buckley

Who was the actress of whom it was said that she ran the whole gamut of her emotions from A to B? Shelley Winters does that. Only in her case she has already taken us through the alphabet twice and is setting out on the third time round. For Miss Winters is the original, genuine Helzapoppin performer and John Kane's play last night enabled her to show her talent to the full.

The play itself was neither here nor there. We have had the lonely heart panting for a gigolo before. The part itself was neither here nor there. We have had actresses playing time-worn actresses before. What mattered was the opportunity the play and the part gave Miss Winters. She clasped it to her bosom.

The effect was electric. The character was created on the instant. From the moment when she first minced across the room and snatched the telephone to give her agent a piece of her mind she was all Hollywood in a London apartment. She was Mae West and Marilyn Monroe. But still the wonder grew. For again and again throughout the play she stood back from the character she had created to add unexpected touches.

She was joined by David Wood. He played a young English fan who came to pray, remained to scoff and nearly lost his virginity in between. His was a splendid performance,

too. He did all that could have been asked of him. But what chance had he against Miss Winters? He spoke, but we looked at her.

"Your dance on the Statue of Liberty is one of my earliest memories", the young man cooed. The face from a thousand billboards searched the past for the occasion he meant. "Of course, when I first saw your films I was too young to be sexually aroused", he protested. "I was only five." For a second the celebrity stared at the age gap. Then the female decided to ignore it.

So it went on. It scarcely mattered that just here and there the action faltered so that you felt the young man would have got out while the going was good. Miss Winters swept the whole thing along in her all-embracing arms. Spurts of panic when the boy rose to go were mingled with moments of sardonic contempt for him and for herself.

The trouble with this overwhelming performance was that inevitably you longed for it to end. For you could not be detached. When the randy creature Miss Winters had built up for us hurried to a drawer for dirty pictures with which to stir her visitor's passion you shuddered for yourself. When she pawed him she was pawing you. It was all too real. So all too soon, like the young man himself, you were desperately looking round for the exit. I do not know how others felt when this ample, diamond-dripping, all-American Delila was wrestling with her reluctant suitor to get him into the bedroom. But she scared the pants off me.

The Vamp: The Times *review.*

The Vamp: *The card from Shelley, given to me before she returned to the USA.*

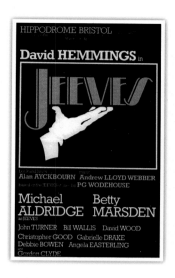

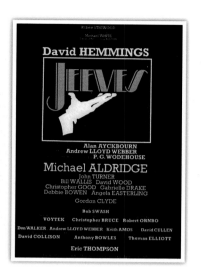

Jeeves: *Bristol flyer, including
Betty Marsden, whose role
was sadly cut for London.*

Jeeves: *The London credits.*

Jeeves: *L to R – Bingo Little (me), Honoria Glossop
(Angela Easterling), Bertie Wooster (David Hemmings), Madeline
Bassett (Gabrielle Drake), Gussie Fink-Nottle (Christopher Good).*

Jeeves: *In my tennis shorts, with the ladies.*

Jeeves: *A staged farewell.* L to R – Jeeves (Michael Aldridge), Dawkins (Jini Steel), Seppings (Graham Hamilton), Ramsay (Elaine Louden), Bertie Wooster (David Hemmings), Sir Watkyn Bassett (Bill Wallis), Honoria Glossop (Angela Easterling), Bingo Little (me), Cropper (Brett Forrest).

Aces High: *The team photo: me with Peter Firth cross-legged, sitting L to R – Trevor Howard, Ray Milland, Richard Johnson, Jacques Maury. Standing L to R – David Daker, Malcolm McDowell, Simon Ward, Christopher Plummer, Tim Pigott-Smith, Ron Pember.*

Aces High: *Me in my flying jacket.*

Aces High: *Peter Firth and me on location in our Royal Flying Corps uniform.*

Aces High: *Caravan shared with Peter Firth.*

Aces High: *2nd Lt. Croft (Peter Firth) and 2nd Lt. 'Tommy' Thompson (me).*

Aces High: *Peter Firth camping it up with our wardrobe friend.*

Aces High: *Newspaper advertisement.*

Aces High: *Meeting Her Majesty in the line-up at the Royal Première with Richard Johnson alongside me.*

some lovely moments and interplay with Bertie Wooster, Jeeves and the hearty, sporty Honoria Glossop, his latest crush. He took part in a comic tennis match, in which he was thrashed by Sir Roderick Spode, the terrifying leader of the fascist organisation, the Black Shorts. I much enjoyed Alan's description of the imposing exterior of Totleigh Towers, which revolved to reveal the rooms inside, decorated in what one imagined would be exquisite period detail, like a giant antique dolls' house.

Before rehearsals began, Andrew invited me to his house in Eaton Square, where he introduced me to my songs, including 'Today', the powerful waltz I had been given as the show's main love song. It had a frighteningly wide range, like many of Andrew's songs, but I hoped I could do it justice. I still have the cassette of the music I recorded that day, complete with Andrew's enthusiastic singing and spoken commentary.

On the first day of rehearsal we assembled, with an air of nervous excitement, at the London Welsh Centre in the Gray's Inn Road. The large gathering included the exuberant Angela Easterling, who was to play opposite me, plus Christopher Good, Gabrielle Drake, Gordon Clyde and Debbie Bowen, who were to play the other couples, David Hemmings and Michael Aldridge, brilliantly cast as Jeeves. I sat next to John Turner, the imposing actor who was to play Roderick Spode. John was one of the few in the cast I already knew. As a student, I had met him and watched several of his impressive performances with the Meadow Players, the resident professional company at the Oxford Playhouse. Opposite us sat the creatives with Bob Swash, the Executive Producer. Apparently Robert Stigwood and Michael White, the two lead producers, were both in America.

Eric warmly welcomed us and gave an introductory talk. He admitted that he had never before directed a musical, and that Andrew and Alan had never created a musical on this scale. Andrew's *Joseph* had started as a short cantata for Colet Court

Preparatory School and *Superstar* had started as an album. But, Eric assured us, we were in safe hands, particularly with the musical expertise of Anthony Bowles, and the choreographic skills of Christopher Bruce, who had created the dance moves for *Joseph*.

Eric then made two comments that caused John and me to exchange worried looks. First, he said that he had been offered six weeks to rehearse the show but had decided to reduce this to four, in the belief that we would all get bored working for longer. Four weeks seemed, particularly for those of us who had done musicals before, woefully little time in which to rehearse a brand-new show. Second, he announced that the first week of rehearsal would be used for blocking, and that we would start learning our songs in week two. Again, this sounded foolhardy. The usual practice for a musical is to get the songs under the belt as soon as possible. Later in the day, Anthony approached us individually, and told us not to worry. He had arranged for several pianos to be installed in basement rooms, with pianists who would secretly teach us the songs whenever we were not needed in Eric's rehearsal upstairs.

A further shock came when Voytek, the noted designer, showed us his set model. Instead of a naturalistic revolving dolls' house, we saw a green box, a minimalist set to which odd pieces of furniture would be added as the story progressed. His concept, it seemed, was that Jeeves would help Bertie tell his story by gradually arranging for more props and pieces of set to be added, as part of the action. This was a clever notion, taking into account the fact that the musical started with Bertie playing his banjo at a concert. The strings of his instrument break, causing him to fill in by telling a story. The resourceful Jeeves does his best to help bring the story to theatrical life. For an experimental production this device might have seemed extremely clever, but perhaps a big West End musical needed to be more spectacular.

The read-through was enjoyable. David's Bertie was endearing, and it was clear that Michael Aldridge was the perfect Jeeves. Bill

Wallis was terrific as the irascible Sir Watkyn Bassett, and the splendid Betty Marsden excelled as Aunt Dahlia, a typical example of a Wodehouse battleaxe. But the show was inescapably too long. It was as though Alan had written a full-length play, to which the songs had been added.

Towards the end of the read-through, Eric interrupted to tell me that this was the moment when I would be flying in upside down from the chandelier. I thought he was joking, but, seeing my surprise, he said surely my agent had told me. I shook my head.

Rehearsals began. Eric decreed that only the actors directly involved in a scene should be in the rehearsal room. In my experience this was unusual. Most directors want all the cast to be involved in the process of putting together the show. An ensemble feeling is created. Everyone can understand and hopefully share the director's vision. But, for the initial days of blocking the scenes, Eric didn't want anyone in the room who was not directly involved. Some of us, waiting to be called, gathered in the surprisingly large entrance hall, furnished with leather armchairs. We used the time to get to know one another. I particularly enjoyed chatting to Betty, whose appearance in the West End revue *On the Brighter Side*, in which she co-starred with Stanley Baxter, was a highlight of my teenage theatre-going. I had also been a huge fan of the radio shows *Beyond Our Ken* and *Round the Horne*, in which she shone during the sixties. She told me that one of the reasons for accepting the role in *Jeeves* was that her husband had recently died and she really needed to work, to distract her from the shock.

Summoned to block my first scene, I found David and Michael in the marked-out area representing the stage. Eric introduced me to the stage management team sitting at tables facing the action. I carried my script, with pencil poised in readiness for instructions. I assumed that, like many directors I had worked with, Eric had pre-planned a basic blocking, so I was surprised when he asked where I would like to enter from. I thought this was a trick question, but remembering that in the scene I was returning from a game of tennis, I asked Eric where the tennis court was. He shrugged his shoulders, saying he hadn't a clue where the tennis court was, but where would I like to come on from. Seeing that David was sitting right of centre, I suggested I might come on from downstage left. Eric said that was fine, and called to the Deputy Stage Manager, in charge of the prompt book, that Mr Wood would be entering from downstage left. From then on I realised that we actors had the freedom to experimentally work out our moves ourselves. This was quite liberating, and I appreciated the fact that we were contributing to the creative process. But it did mean that the process took quite a long time, and didn't lead to concrete decisions being made. Progress, therefore, was slow, and by the end of the first week of rehearsal we still had not succeeded in blocking the whole show. Meanwhile, we engaged in our clandestine sessions downstairs, learning the songs.

Some scenes proved particularly tricky to make work. I remember the Spode versus Bingo tennis match never felt as funny acted out as it appeared on the page. The mighty John Turner smashed imaginary tennis balls over an imaginary net, causing me as Bingo to fall and flounder helplessly on the ground. Such unsubtle slapstick felt wrong for Wodehouse.

My feet were another problem. My dance skills have always been modest, to say the least. And they had not been tested at my audition. The ever-patient Christopher Bruce did his best to teach me to waltz gracefully with the ladies during my 'Today' number. I'm sure he had to simplify his intended choreography, but I like to think that the end result was presentable, partly because my tennis shorts gave the sequence comic effect and partly because a falling shower of rose petals distracted the audience from concentrating on my two left feet.

I don't remember much rewriting going on during rehearsal, although Alan made occasional visits. But one day Andrew confided in me that he didn't feel a song was working. He intended to replace it with a very bouncy tune from *Dr Barnardo* he had played to me in Oxford. Alan provided new lyrics and 'Travel Hopefully' was the result. Several of us subsequently provided offstage backing vocals for this catchy number.

During the first two weeks of rehearsal I was surprised that I wasn't called all day every day. In my free time I was able to catch up on other projects. The producer Cameron Mackintosh and I were presenting my children's musical *The Owl and the Pussycat Went to See…* I was able to attend its opening performance at the Westminster Theatre. Cameron was also producing *Rock Nativity*, the musical I wrote with Tony Hatch, which had had a successful opening Christmas season in Newcastle. Now there were meetings about its proposed tour. I also fitted in a job recording the commentary for a BBC documentary about Nijinsky.

At the end of week three of rehearsal I was sent to Her Majesty's Theatre for my first and only flying practice. There was no show up and running, presumably because they were waiting for *Jeeves* to arrive. So the stage was empty, a Kirby's flying mechanism had been rigged and Inky, a veteran operator, who had flown several celebrated Peter Pans in his career, welcomed me and fitted me into a two-wire harness. I was in safe hands. Later I discovered that Inky was paid considerably more than me per week, which was reassuring. As I rose high above the stage, the pressure on my nether regions was not as uncomfortable as I had feared, and Inky even encouraged me to look graceful as I flew back and forth. But I was relieved that there was as yet no sign of the chandelier from which I was to hang upside down.

The following Saturday morning we had our first stagger through the whole show. This was attended by Bob Swash, Andrew, Alan and other members of the production team, including Robert Ornbo and David Collison, the respected lighting designer and sound designer respectively. By coincidence I knew them both.

They were part of Theatre Projects, the theatre consultants, whose supremo Richard Pilbrow, had employed me to write the screenplay for *Swallows and Amazons* (1974). Robert and David were often in the office when I attended meetings.

Before we took a deep breath and began to run the show, Eric suggested that we all take part in a sweepstake. The idea was that we would all write down our estimate of the production's running time and make a modest financial contribution to the kitty. Whoever guessed nearest the running time would win the money. This presented us with a dilemma. Should we be loyal to the production and suggest a trim two and a half hours including interval or should we be honest and reckon on more than four hours? In the end, Christopher Good won the prize with an estimate of three hours forty minutes. It had been a long morning. Dispirited, leaving the creatives to conduct a post-mortem, many of the cast retreated to the pub over the road, where we discussed what measures might be taken to shorten the show. We only had a week's rehearsal left before departing for Bristol, where the show was due to open its pre-London run.

After a worried weekend, we all nervously assembled, anticipating a very large pair of scissors, but Eric surprised us by applying to the script a very small pair of nail scissors, cutting half a line here and half a line there. He told us not to worry. The run-through had been extremely slow. If the ten principals simply speeded up their performance, each could lose about five minutes, which would save fifty minutes of running time. Incredulous faces greeted this announcement. But rehearsals resumed and we all did our best to remain positive.

By the time we arrived in Bristol we had become a very close-knit company of actors. We all tried to conceal our concerns and support each other with humour and team spirit. Indeed, it was suggested, with tongue-in-cheek cynicism, that we should strike a veterans' medal and all wear it to commemorate the war we had come through together. But it was a real pleasure to leave London for a change of scene, and install ourselves within the magnificent Hippodrome. Our spirits were raised by the ornate Matcham auditorium, and the sound of the orchestra – I seem to remember there were fifty musicians – gave us fresh hope and enthusiasm. The male chorus of The Drones sounded great and tap danced most effectively. And the lush orchestrations enhanced Andrew's lovely tunes. Singing 'Half a Moment' in the finale always gave me a glow of pleasure. We had no radio mics in those days. Balancing our voices against the orchestra must have been quite a task for David Collison.

Technical rehearsals rarely run smoothly or exactly according to plan. Different departments with individual expertise finally assemble in the theatre and rapidly must form a cooperative team. The actors, hopefully having become proficient in their lines and moves, are suddenly confronted with costumes, scenery, lighting and sound, and must patiently become puppets, just one component in what needs to become a smoothly running machine. With musicals the challenge is even greater, with the actors learning to cope with orchestral arrangements instead of the piano accompaniment they are used to in rehearsals. Time is at a premium, too, as the first night approaches. The director's daunting task, as captain of the ship, is to maintain a steady course through what can be extremely choppy waters. *Jeeves* was opening on the Thursday evening. The get-in rigging and lighting preparations took place on the Sunday and Monday. Meanwhile, we actors settled into our dressing rooms and had final costume fittings. On Tuesday rehearsals began and we actors first set foot onstage. The first hurdle, I remember, was Voytek's green box. It was made of solid wood and stretched across the back of the stage, then down each side to the front. There were doors through which to make entrances. But the wooden walls were so thick that, when standing in the wings, we found it very difficult to hear our cues from onstage. We would stand, ears pressed tightly against the wall, listening hard. I seem to remember that cue lights had to be provided to facilitate some entrances.

When not involved in a scene, I sometimes sat in the stalls to watch proceedings. One scene illustrated the problems caused by the design concept. David and Betty, as Bertie and Aunt Dahlia, had an argument in what in the script had been an elegant drawing room. To persuade Bertie to do her bidding, Aunt Dahlia threw priceless figurines into the fireplace until Bertie agreed to her demands. But there was no drawing room. There was no fireplace. In the centre of the stage, surrounded by the green box, was a chaise longue and a small table, on which stood three or four white plaster figures that bore no resemblance to the antique knick-knacks suggested in the script. Betty came to the moment where she should start lobbing them into the fireplace. She hesitated. From the director's desk in the stalls, Eric suggested she throw one on the floor. She did. It smashed to smithereens, scattering broken bits and a cloud of dust over the stage. There was a long delay as stage management tidied up the mess. I can't remember if or how the situation was resolved, but even Betty, one of the most skilled comediennes of her generation, couldn't be expected to raise a laugh with this clumsy bit of business.

As the day wore on, progress was slow. Tension mounted. In those days, Equity's regulation about rehearsal time limits were not as strict as now, so we found ourselves continuing late into the night. We came to the point where David had to pull on a bell rope and unexpectedly rise into the air, with Inky, the other side of the wall, acting as a counterweight. David was reluctant to attempt this bit of business so late in the day, whereupon Eric undiplomatically accused him of cowardice. This went down badly, and although David managed to keep his cool, the atmosphere throughout the theatre became strained, to say the least.

On Wednesday we started and stopped our way through Act 1, but by late evening had still not reached the interval. As more and more technical problems arose and had to be resolved as best as possible, I don't think I was alone in developing a sinking feeling in my stomach. At one point I found myself sitting next to David in the wings on a small set of steps on castors. 'We're not going to be ready, are we?' David said. I agreed. 'Well,' said David, 'if Michael Crawford can delay the opening of *Billy* in Manchester, I can do it for *Jeeves*.' Brave words, but David didn't act on them. We carried on, in the hope that things would improve.

Before I left the theatre that night, I was asked to come in early the next morning – the morning of the day we were due to open. I was asked to get into my black tie evening dress, ready for a flying rehearsal. I had noticed the chandelier up high in the flies, and spent a sleepless night in anticipation of the challenge that lay ahead. Sleep had, in fact, been something of a problem since arriving in Bristol. My room in the digs had rats, or maybe large mice, in the ceiling, who scuttled regularly and noisily from one side to the other.

The next morning, I put on my immaculate suit. All the male principals had been provided with tailor-made evening dress. We also had specially made pink hunting costumes, which in the end were never used. As I arrived in the wings, I realised I should have waited for Inky to help me on with my flying harness. This had to fit under the suit. The wardrobe department hadn't realised this, and we discovered that my suit was too well-fitting to accommodate it. A larger suit was miraculously hired at great speed from the local branch of Moss Bros. Holes had to be cut into the sides of the trousers to allow the wires to be attached. Finally we were ready. Inky hoisted me way up high over the stage-right wing, then pulled me across to a position over the centre of the stage, above the waiting chandelier. This proved to be a tricky manoeuvre. Dangling helplessly, I had to negotiate my way through lighting bars and various wires. I remember calling out, 'I feel like a piece of cheese!' To my shame, for the first and only time in my life, I completely freaked out and screamed to be let down. After being given a strong brandy in David Hemmings's dressing room, I was immensely relieved to be told that this moment would be cut from the show until we reached London.

We didn't manage to finish the technical rehearsal. And there was certainly no time for a full dress rehearsal. Instead we prepared, with understandable anxiety, for our first night.

We survived our ordeal, and it is fair to say that the audience reaction was more positive than we had feared. The show still felt uneven and unwieldy, but the tunefulness of the songs, the complications of the plot and the quality of the performances seemed to gain approval. David Harrison, the local critic, enjoyed The Drones linking the scenes in song, and praised 'the hilarious pseudo-patriotic S.P.O.D.E.' as 'a marvellous set piece'. He rightly considered Michael Aldridge 'a perfect Jeeves' and wrote, 'Bill Wallis was a marvellous Sir Watkyn Bassett – absolutely in character, as was Christopher Good as Gussie Fink-Nottle and Gabrielle Drake (Madeline).' But he felt that David was too intelligent as Bertie and that Betty was wasted as Aunt Dahlia. He ended his review by saying, 'the play is being premiered in Bristol before moving to the West End. I hope by then it can be pruned to well under the three hours mark, and it should have a mildly successful run.' The show was indeed far too long. I remember hearing the sound of seats tipping back as audience members left not long after the interval. At first I thought it was because they didn't like the show, but then realised they were escaping to catch their last buses. Curtain up had been at 8pm, and we were still going strong, or not so strong, at 11.30pm.

We had assumed that during our two-week run in Bristol, more cuts would be introduced. But for the first few days nothing changed. It was rumoured that Andrew refused to cut any of the music until Alan cut some of the dialogue, and that Alan refused to cut any of the dialogue until Andrew cut some of the music. Eric, apparently, refused to cut anything until the writers gave him instructions. Michael Aldridge, it was reported, walked along the corridors of the creatives' hotel late at night knocking on doors and calling, 'Please talk to one another – we have to do it, you know!'

Eventually, in a foolhardy attempt to move the situation on, David called a crisis meeting. This involved Michael, Gabrielle, David and myself. It was secretly arranged that we should meet early next morning in David's hotel room. David was determined to find a way to break the deadlock. I arrived early from my digs, and decided to treat myself to breakfast in the hotel dining room. Suddenly, to my embarrassment, Alan and his partner Heather Stoney appeared, expressed pleasurable surprise at my presence, and joined me at the table. I could hardly reveal the reason for my visit, so lamely explained I just fancied a good breakfast. Heather and I had acted together in Alan's *Me Times Me Times Me*, so I much enjoyed meeting her again. And Alan had always been very friendly. Feeling disloyal, I left them at the appointed hour and made my way upstairs. David's suggestion was that we should somehow lock the management, the director and the creatives out of the theatre while the cast endeavoured to improve the show by cutting it down to size. David would take over direction. I would be in charge of rewrites. Michael and Gabrielle would be in charge of diplomacy. David agreed to set the wheels in motion.

Our planned takeover never happened. But whatever David said to the powers that be led to a full company meeting, at which everybody could have their say. Eric led the meeting and didn't appear too worried about our concerns. Several people were brave enough to question certain aspects of the production, as well as its extreme length. In retrospect, I was foolish to suggest that one solution might be to cut the sub-plot involving Bingo and Honoria. It was true that Bingo featured hardly at all in Wodehouse's *The Code of the Woosters*, on which much of our play was based, and Honoria featured not at all. But I was wrong to suggest such a cut, and unfair to Angela, who played Honoria. It might have been permissible to suggest cutting my character, but not hers. Eric, quite rightly, tore me off a strip, saying that just because I did a bit of writing as well as acting, I had no right, as an actor in the show, to criticise the writing. Put firmly in my place, I shut up.

But the meeting had at least brought out into the open the general disquiet within the company, and subsequently a few changes were made. Most cruel was the decision to cut the role of Aunt Dahlia completely. This undeniably helped the structure and running time of the show, but was a devastating blow for Betty, still recovering from the death of her husband. We were all very sorry to see her go.

Cuts were rehearsed to accommodate Aunt Dahlia's departure. Then Andrew asked me to meet him at the theatre to try out a new introduction to my 'Today' song. The next morning, I arrived onstage and was surprised to see the entire orchestra assembled in the pit. Paul Maguire, the assistant musical director, welcomed me. Andrew took me to the grand piano at the back of the stalls to teach me his new composition. Meanwhile, he suggested that the orchestra should have a coffee break. They all left the pit. The new introduction was only eight or sixteen bars long, and didn't take long to learn. Andrew and I went through it several times, then waited for the orchestra to return. Then Paul took up his baton and the orchestra accompanied my singing. I remember thinking how impressive it was that the new introduction had been fully arranged. After a few run-throughs, Andrew said that soon Eric and Bob would arrive to hear the new intro and decide on whether it should replace the old one. Meanwhile, Andrew suggested that the orchestra should go for another coffee break. Fifteen minutes later they reassembled and Eric and Bob, together with, as I remember, Bob's assistant, Lee Menzies, sat in the stalls and listened. I sang the new intro a couple of times. There was a brief discussion, after which I was told that everyone preferred the original intro. It was to stay in. I was thanked for coming, and that was it. Heaven knows how much this brief experiment cost. It struck me how much respect Andrew clearly commanded to be allowed to call such an expensive workshop.

In our second Bristol week more changes were made, but nothing major. One evening I was in my dressing room as the orchestra started tuning up for the overture. There was a knock on the door. In came Hugh Wooldridge, Eric's amiable assistant. 'Message from Eric,' he said hastily. 'First scene. No tennis racquet.' I asked Hugh to explain, and he simply repeated that Eric didn't want me to use my tennis racquet in my first scene. He left the room. I quickly went through the scene in my mind. Occasionally, during my conversation with Bertie, I practised the odd tennis stroke to add emphasis to a line. No problem, I thought, I can just mime the strokes. But it seemed odd that I shouldn't be carrying my racquet, having just returned from the tennis court. As the overture began, I suddenly remembered that during the scene Michael, as Jeeves, silently approached me and gently adjusted my grip on the racquet. This bit of business had arisen spontaneously in rehearsal, was quite fun, and it seemed appropriate that Jeeves, possessing all-round knowledge, should unobtrusively offer Bingo assistance. I realised that Michael must be warned that I would be racquet-less. He was the first person onstage following the overture. So I hurtled down several flights of stone steps, rushed up to Michael, standing waiting in the wings and urgently shouted over the sound of the orchestra, 'No racquet! Eric says no racquet!' Without reacting, Michael walked onstage and the performance began.

When I came on for my first scene with Bertie, I waved my invisible racquet around instead of the real thing. David gave me a puzzled look, clearly thinking I had forgotten the racquet. At the usual point in the scene, Michael, with great aplomb, approached and adjusted my grip, as though I was holding the real racquet. He even managed to give me a wink, in a deadpan moment of complicity. I treasured that moment.

The next day, with no explanation, I was asked to reinstate the racquet.

As the Bristol run came towards a close, we didn't seem much further on. A few adjustments were in place, but the show was still very long. A group of us cast members went out to tea, accompanied by Anthony Bowles, our musical director. As we confided our misgivings, he, perhaps surprisingly, as one of the creatives, agreed that we were nowhere near ready for the West End. Disloyally, but honestly, we reluctantly reckoned that if there were any justice in the British theatre, the show would not get positive reviews. But we recognised that the critics and the first-night audience might be blinded by the impressive combination of Wodehouse, Ayckbourn, Lloyd Webber and Thompson, and we could find ourselves in a hit musical. Wishful thinking, perhaps, but not an impossible scenario.

I have often wondered what was going on in the minds of the creatives. Were they as concerned as us? Surely they must have been. But, quite rightly, they knew their duty was to inspire confidence in the cast and, perhaps, as the juggernaut rolled on, it was impossible to change course. There was still no sign of our producers, Robert Stigwood and Michael White, and Bob Swash, the executive producer, was such a pleasant man that perhaps he lacked the authority to steer the creative team more persuasively.

David Collison, the sound designer, in his very readable memoir *Namedropping in the Wings*, succinctly summed up the situation:

I remember being in a pub with Robert Ornbo one lunchtime when worried members of the cast including David Hemmings were agreeing about scenes that should be cut and how the plot could be altered to improve the story. It was all so obvious, why could the director and the production team not see it? One hoped that Hemmings, who had a lot riding on the success of this, his first musical, would insist on the changes. But he was far too nice. Everybody on that production was nice, and nobody wanted to upset Eric Thompson because he was so nice. One would have thought that experienced writer and director Alan Ayckbourn would have intervened, but he is also terribly nice. Unfortunately the producers were not in evidence. Had they been there to witness the chaos, there would surely have been fireworks. They had entrusted the production to a colleague, a most likeable and charming man, but not one who relished confrontations or making tough decisions. He was too nice.

We all returned to London and the production was installed in Her Majesty's Theatre. Our first preview was the following Friday. Once the set was up, we had the photo-call. It was taken by no less than Patrick, Lord Lichfield, the eminent fashion photographer. In a lengthy session he took individual black-and-white photos of us all to be used front of house, and artistically staged colour images of scenes from the show, beautifully lit, for the glossy souvenir programme. Lord Lichfield was a delight to pose for, and his results were enchanting.

News came that a solution had been found to facilitate my chandelier acrobatics. A special walkway had been built from the wings stage right, high up in the flies. An assistant stage manager accompanied me up the stairs and fixed the two wires to the attachment on the harness. When a green light flashed, I literally walked the plank! I sensed the tension on the wires tighten as Inky supported me and edged me further across. Having arrived at the centre, hanging in mid-air, I was lowered onto the chandelier, latched the back of my legs onto a branch, and dangled upside down waiting to be lowered with the chandelier down into the view of the audience. We rehearsed this calmly and methodically, thanks to Inky, in whom I had complete trust. I summoned up the courage to do it every performance, and eventually rather enjoyed it. Sadly, the Gallery First Nighters, when criticising the moment in the play, didn't appreciate my bravery. And why should they?

The technical rehearsal was smoother than in Bristol, and we achieved a full dress rehearsal. The show was now running at just over three hours. Still too long.

My most vivid memory of the previews was Eric coming to my dressing room with a piece of paper, on which were written two new verses for my 'Today' song, which he asked me to learn and substitute for the existing verses the next night. I read them and told him that, quite frankly, I didn't think they were very good. With the best will in the world, I felt that Alan's rewrites weren't as good as the originals. Eric flinched. 'I wrote those words,' he said. 'Alan didn't want to.' Oh dear. I had put my foot in it again. I said I would do my best to learn the words, but wasn't sure if I could be ready to perform them the next night. He insisted, and left the room.

In the song, Bingo, my character, wandered round, explaining his philosophy of romantically living in the moment to his friend Bertie, who listened sitting down. I told David I might struggle to learn the new lines in time. He typically offered to help. Both of us had several times talked about our interest in conjuring. David suggested he might palm a card with one verse written on it, which I could use as a crib sheet by looking over his shoulder. The other verse I wrote on my hand. By slightly changing my moves and occasionally glancing down, it was possible to sing the song with confidence. But for two or three performances, until the words were under my belt, I felt embarrassed to be cheating this way on a West End stage. But David's magical expertise was much appreciated.

On the Saturday night before our opening press performance the following Thursday, just before the beginners' call, Keith Percival's voice echoed from the dressing-room tannoy, calling us all immediately to the large chorus dressing room at the top of the theatre. We all trooped upstairs. The orchestra was tuning up. The show was about to start. What was happening? Eric appeared, brandishing his trademark cigarette holder and holding a glass of white wine. Barely holding back his emotions, he told us that the management had informed him that the production was ninety-nine per cent there, but that he was not the person to deliver the remaining one per cent. He thanked us all for our hard work and announced that Alan Ayckbourn would be taking over the direction from now on. He left in silence. It was hard to know whether we were shocked or relieved. But there was no time to discuss the situation with one another. We all hurried back downstairs and the overture began.

In the few remaining days, Alan gently made some changes, but I don't remember them affecting my role very much. And it was probably too late to make major structural alterations.

Early in the morning on our opening Thursday, I had a phone call from Keith, asking me to come into the theatre to meet Alan. No rehearsal had been scheduled for that day, so I was surprised, but travelled in as requested. Alan met me, immaculately dressed. 'Ah!' I exclaimed. 'Your first-night suit!' Alan shook his head and explained, a little agitated, that he was off to Buckingham Palace to have lunch with the Queen. Not the ideal day for this honour, perhaps. He gently informed me that Robert Stigwood, one of the producers, had seen the performance the night before. It was probably the first time he had been to see us. Apparently, after the show, he had decreed that my song, 'Today', should be cut. No explanation was given. The news wasn't much of a confidence-builder, hours before press night. But Alan reassured me, saying that he and Anthony Bowles had told Mr Stigwood that such a cut at such short notice was impossible. Quite apart from the difficulty of making the changes the cut would necessitate, there wouldn't be time to rearrange the sheet music on the musicians' music stands. These reasons didn't seem entirely persuasive, but I was relieved and grateful for the fact that my song had been saved. Alan couldn't guarantee that 'Today' would not be cut in the future, but felt it was only fair for me to be told what had happened, just in case I heard it from another source. I thanked Alan and he set off for his royal lunch.

I received some lovely first-night cards from friends, family and members of the company. Andrew sent a somewhat cryptic note saying, 'It's been a long way since Dr Barnardo, but maybe we would have had to make a lot of changes.' Cameron Mackintosh sent a celebratory bottle. Eric sent a friendly message, and Mr Stigwood rather ironically, sent his 'sincere good wishes and thanks'.

My memory of the first performance is clouded by the boos that greeted my chandelier appearance. But we must have got through it without any disasters. Having said that, the audience reaction was polite rather than ecstatic.

As is customary, friends and well-wishers came backstage after the show. Andrew kindly came to say thank you, and, at the same moment, Cameron arrived at my dressing-room door. I introduced them to each other, and have always been convinced that this was the very first time that they had met. Maybe I am responsible, in a very small way, for their future hugely successful partnership, mounting shows like *Cats* and *The Phantom of the Opera*.

We had all been invited to a first-night party at Mr Stigwood's Elizabethan mansion, The Old Barn, in Harrow. I'm afraid I was one of several who decided not to attend.

The following morning the critics didn't hold back. Michael Billington in the *Guardian* talked of 'This three-hour insult to Wodehouse'. He was sad 'that it may convince people who have never read any Wodehouse that he was a painfully unfunny writer with an elephantine humorous style.' John Barber in the *Telegraph* wrote, 'This disastrous attempt of a parody of 1930s modes and manners misses fire in every single department.' Milton Shulman in the *Evening Standard* enjoyed The Drones, and called Gabrielle Drake and Debbie Bowen 'delectable and amusing'. He recorded my uncomfortable 'big' moment, writing:

Judging from the restive noises in the gallery last night, it was clear that Alan Ayckbourn, as writer of the book and lyrics, had exhausted the patience of much of his audience by the time Bertie had to rescue Bingo Little from a chandelier.

Herbert Kretzmer, in the *Daily Express*, enjoyed some of Andrew's melodies, and David's 'gallant and endearing performance', but his review had the headline, *'Brave Bertie swims, while the rest sink'*. Perhaps B.A. Young in the *Financial Times* made a perceptive point when he wrote:

I have always believed, and I still do, that P.G. Wodehouse's stories can't be properly dramatised. Too much of their character lies in the narrative and the interior monologues of the characters, and in the case of the novels in the complexity of the plots.

I was surprised, and rather flattered, that he ended his review with, 'David Wood in the part of Bingo Little, which seems to have been left in by mistake, gives by far the best performance of the evening'.

The Sunday reviews were similarly discouraging, except for Harold Hobson in *The Sunday Times*. He had thoroughly enjoyed the show, calling it a great example of a musical that correctly goes back to Greece and the throwing of 'rationality to the winds – to rise to a frenzied Dionysiac ecstasy … Jeeves accomplishes this on at least four occasions.' He particularly liked the way David as Bertie sometimes broke the fourth wall, giving as an example the incident when Bertie, 'faced with yet another dismaying contretemps, staggers back appalled, and then turns to the audience, and anxiously says, "I staggered back appalled."' Hobson went on to say, 'At least two critics of undoubted gravity, as well as a small boy of my acquaintance, have admitted to being as enchanted with the glorious irrationality of this episode as I was myself.' The following Sunday, and the Sunday after, Hobson tried to rescue *Jeeves* from the inevitable with further kind reviews. But we all realised that box-office business was very unlikely to be brisk, and that soon we would receive notice that the production would close. In the event, we survived for six weeks, mainly because the theatre owners agreed to give time to Robert Stigwood to put together a revival of *Hair* to replace us, and this couldn't be done immediately. So we carried on, playing to ever dwindling audience numbers. But by now the company had become galvanised into a resilient team, and we were determined to enjoy our work, even if the show was still running at longer than three hours.

Before the curtain finally came down, three memorable events took place. First, we recorded the cast album. Despite the show's demise, Andrew's recording company decided to press ahead. Maybe this was thanks to the huge sales of the *Jesus Christ Superstar* album. We had an exciting experience working at the famous Olympic Studios in Barnes. Anthony Bowles conducted the sessions over two days. I remember I had difficulty reaching the very high note at the end of 'Today'. Anthony patiently let me repeat the final sequence several times, and the engineers successfully spliced a reasonable take to the rest of the track. The resulting album, expertly produced, became a lasting souvenir to treasure.

A few days later, I was enthusiastically talking about it to Tony Hatch, the composer of 'Downtown' and many other popular hits. Tony had rather unfairly become known as 'the Hatchet Man', as a result of his honest appraisals of some of the acts featured in the television talent show *New Faces*. Tony and I had been working on our musical *Rock Nativity*. He is one of the nicest people I have ever worked with, and had invited me to a music awards ceremony in a posh Park Lane hotel. As we chatted in the foyer, Andrew happened to arrive. Tony and Andrew had never met, so I introduced them. Tony's other recent musical, *The Card*, produced by Cameron Mackintosh at the Queen's Theatre, had recently suffered a similar fate to *Jeeves*, forced to close early. Sympathetically, Tony said to

Andrew, 'Sorry about Jeeves.' Andrew stiffened. 'Well,' he replied, 'there was nothing wrong with the music. And the cast album will become a collector's item.' With that, he walked away. His reply may have been unnecessarily abrupt, but of course he was proved right. Any attempt today to find a copy of the album online won't be easy, and a positive result will be eye-wateringly expensive.

Next, my chandelier moment had one more surprise in store. One night, as I walked up the stage-left wings, before crossing the stage behind the set and climbing the stairs to get ready for my flight, I passed the splendid Inky. He had just completed the bell rope cue, in which he acted as a counterbalance with David. This operation had gone wrong, and Inky had been lifted in the air and had hit his head hard on a strut projecting from a piece of scenery. Blood was pouring from his head. Naturally I found this a little worrying, and, having reached my special walkway, and as my wires were attached to me and I awaited the green light, I prayed that Inky still had the strength to support me. The cue came, I felt the tension on the wires, I walked into space and was lowered onto the chandelier as usual. Then, as I hung upside down, I heard the loud screech of an ambulance siren speeding down Haymarket. Next, I felt myself lowered down to be rescued by David. All went well. But by the time I came offstage, Inky had collapsed, unconscious, and was in the ambulance on his way to hospital. What a professional he was! What a hero! I remember him with eternal gratitude.

The third memorable event came a couple of weeks before our final performance. At the end of the show we were asked to wait in the wings before returning to our dressing rooms. Suddenly Michael White appeared. He was the second lead producer of *Jeeves*, who had just returned from the United States. Presumably he had just seen the production for the first time. He graciously thanked us all for our hard work and apologised for not having been available before. He said that he was sure we were all aware of the fact that the show was too long. He implied that if it was half an hour or so shorter, the show wouldn't necessarily be better, but it would at least be shorter and therefore more acceptable to the audience. Alan, he said, had returned to Scarborough. Andrew had apparently gone to Barbados. Would we, the cast, be willing to organise and implement the necessary cuts ourselves? His question was greeted at first with silence. Mr White asked us to consider the idea, then left. Bill Wallis, I remember, in character as Sir Watkyn Bassett, angrily spoke against us agreeing to take on this responsibility. But David, ever our pragmatic leader, thought we should have a go. We had all regularly discussed the length problem ourselves, and even come up with our own ideas of cuts. Several of us nodded our agreement, and finally it was decided we would all come in next day and see what might happen. Needless to say, within a couple of hours we had harmoniously cut about twenty-five minutes off the running time, without any member of the cast complaining that he or she had lost their favourite bit. The cuts were introduced, and our final performances had a healthier running time of about two and a half hours including interval.

As we said our last-night goodbyes, it was with mixed feelings. Relief, certainly. But we all felt like close comrades, who had battled our way through an unforgettable experience. I'm sure most of us would say that our careers were not adversely affected by taking part in *Jeeves*. As for the creatives, Andrew went on to have unparalleled success in musical theatre, and Alan regularly reinforced his reputation as one of our greatest living playwrights. Indeed, only a month after *Jeeves* closed, Alan opened *Bedroom Farce* in Scarborough. This play was to become one of his major successes.

Later the same year, 1975, Eric directed Alan's *The Norman Conquests* on Broadway. And his production of Alan's *Absurd Person Singular* was still running in New York a year later. Eric died, aged fifty-three, in 1982. I remember him fondly, even though perhaps he was out of his depth directing a big musical. I always think of him when seeing on-screen his talented wife, Phyllida Law, and daughters, the Oscar-winning (now a Dame) Emma Thompson and Olivier Award-winning Sophie Thompson, whom I had the pleasure of directing on a British Drama League summer course, when she was aged about fourteen.

Anthony Bowles went on to musically direct the Lloyd Webber/ Rice great success, *Evita*, in 1978 but sadly died in 1993 at the age of sixty-one.

Choreographer Christopher Bruce achieved great acclaim as the Artistic Director of Ballet Rambert.

Bob Swash lived until the age of ninety-one. He produced *Evita*, as well as Willy Russell's hits, *John, Paul, George, Ringo ... and Bert, Blood Brothers* and *Shirley Valentine*.

Voytek, the designer, who was already a very successful television designer who, unusually, had a simultaneous career as a television director, would win a Critics' Circle Theatre Award for his design for Botho Strauss's *Great and Small* at the Vaudeville Theatre and his second BAFTA for the London Weekend Television miniseries *Dandelion Dead*. He died, aged eighty-nine, in 2014.

David Collison became the leading sound engineer of his generation, and Robert Ornbo remained for many years one of our most brilliant lighting designers. I was privileged to work with him again when I directed my children's play *Save the Human*. Sitting next to him in the auditorium as he put the cues into the lighting board was like attending a masterclass.

Andrew must have retained a firm belief in the possibilities of a Wodehouse musical, and twenty years later a completely reworked *Jeeves*, entitled *By Jeeves*, played a try-out season in Scarborough. Alan was back on board, and together they reworked the idea, rewrote book, lyrics and songs, trimmed the cast and orchestra numbers, and produced a much more successful version. In 1996, Alan directed it for the West End, featuring Steven Pacey and Malcolm Sinclair, at the Duke of York's Theatre, from where it subsequently transferred to the Lyric Theatre. Alan later directed it on Broadway, with Martin Jarvis as Jeeves. And Andrew's faith was duly vindicated. Very few of the original songs remain, and my 'Today' survived only as a short section of incidental music.

In the intervening years, Andrew had raided his original *Jeeves* score and some of it reappeared in his other musicals. 'Summer Day' was reworked into 'Another Suitcase in Another Hall' for *Evita*. The melody of 'Literary Men' reappeared in *Song and Dance*, first as the finale song, 'When You Want to Fall in Love', and later in the first act as the haunting 'Unexpected Song'. The introduction to 'Half a Moment' became the middle eight of 'As If We Never Said Goodbye' in *Sunset Boulevard*.

To my knowledge, David Hemmings never played another stage role. He continued to co-star in films, including Ken Russell's *The Rainbow* and Ridley Scott's *Gladiator*. He developed a career as a television and film director, at first in Australia. In the 1980s he relocated to Hollywood and worked consistently until his death aged sixty-two in 2003.

To me, and, I'm sure, to my fellow *Jeeves* cast members, he will ever remain the hero of *Tottering Towers*.

PLAYING AN ACE

1976

Aces High starring Malcolm
McDowell and Christopher Plummer

Reunited after a decade with Malcolm McDowell, my fellow rebel schoolboy in Lindsay Anderson's If…., *I found myself in Royal Flying Corps uniform filming* Aces High, *an airborne adaptation of one of my favourite plays, R.C. Sherriff's* Journey's End.

One summer's day in 1975, I found myself sitting cross-legged in a field in Buckinghamshire, wearing the uniform of a Lieutenant in the Royal Flying Corps. Next to me sat Peter Firth, whom I had much admired playing the disturbed teenager Alan in Peter Shaffer's play *Equus* at the National Theatre a couple of years earlier. He had repeated the role on Broadway. To my amazement, sitting on chairs behind me were Hollywood legends, the British actors Ray Milland and Trevor Howard. Both had first reached stardom in 1945, Milland in *The Lost Weekend* and Howard in *Brief Encounter*. Now they were playing cameo roles in the film *Aces High*. We were posing for a publicity team photo. Standing at the back were Malcolm McDowell, with whom I had acted in Lindsay Anderson's *If....* seven years earlier, Simon Ward, the star of Richard Attenborough's *Young Winston* (1972), in the role I unsuccessfully auditioned for, and Christopher Plummer, the Canadian star of the 1965 film, *The Sound of Music*, a credit I later read he rather resented. Also in the picture were Richard Johnson, the distinguished star of many British movies, and Tim Pigott-Smith, a former fellow student with my wife, Jacqueline Stanbury, at the Bristol Old Vic Theatre School. *Aces High* was an Anglo-French film, set in the First World War. It cleverly transposed the story of R.C. Sherriff's stage play *Journey's End* from the trenches to the air. Howard Barker, the screenwriter, had retained and renamed the play's characters and transformed them from British Army infantry officers fighting in France, to brave flying aces whose life expectancy was appallingly short. Malcolm played the commander and Peter was the latest fresh-faced recruit, whose disillusionment provided the through-line of the story. Christopher was the avuncular senior officer, Simon played the coward on the verge of a nervous breakdown, and I was the eternally cheerful one, whose life inevitably came to a tragic end. As a great admirer of Sherriff's play, I was thrilled to get the part.

'Tommy' Thompson was an ideal role for me. It involved singing a couple of songs in the officers' mess, becoming an endearingly eccentric comrade, and being seen to die a grisly death. It was a rewarding part to play. But I nearly turned it down. When the offer came through, I was heavily involved in planning a new musical revue, in which I was to perform and to co-write with John Gould, my regular collaborator. John excelled as a composer and comedian. We had met at Oxford University, writing songs together, producing and appearing in revues and cabaret, and I had directed John's musical *You Can't Do Much Without a Screwdriver*. We had worked together on *Hang Down Your Head and Die*, the anti-capital punishment revue, and *Four Degrees Over*, the musical revue, both of which transferred to the West End. Our proposed new show was to be directed, to our delight, by Ian McKellen. Already highly respected as a classical actor, Ian had successfully turned his hand to directing a double bill by Joe Orton at Watford's Palace Theatre. John had been the musical director. He had then persuaded Ian to direct our new revue. We had had several planning meetings. We had begun booking touring dates. We had started writing. But suddenly I received the invitation to be in *Aces High*. I had a very difficult decision to make. There were sleepless nights and long discussions with John, who insisted that the revue project couldn't go ahead without me. A crunch meeting was organised at Ian McKellen's house. I arrived early, feeling torn and guilty. Discussing my dilemma, I became so distressed that I had to retire to Ian's bathroom to be sick. He, with kind sympathy, helped clean me up, and then John arrived. My eventual decision to join the cast of *Aces High* came as a huge blow to John. It took some time for our friendship and collaboration to recover and resume. Ian, of course, didn't need us. His career trajectory went ever upwards. And it was a relief when John picked up the pieces, appeared as a regular on Esther Rantzen's *That's Life* television programme and created a successful one-man show called *Bars of Gould*, which I co-produced with him. But although the whole affair had left a nasty taste in the mouth for both of us, in retrospect, the decision I made was one I would never regret.

The main reason why I couldn't resist being in *Aces High* was that it gave me the chance to work for the second time with the director Jack Gold. It was a pleasure to meet him again at my interview with the film's co-producer, S. Benjamin Fisz. 'Benny' was an immediately likeable Polish gentleman, who had emigrated to the United Kingdom and become a fighter pilot in the Royal Air Force during the Second World War. Not surprisingly, *Aces High* was a personal pet project, and his passion lit up the interview.

Jack Gold had made his mark as the director of *The National Health* (1973), the film version of the National Theatre play by Peter Nichols, and the award-winning television adaptation of *The Naked Civil Servant*, Quentin Crisp's autobiography. In fact, at the time of my interview, Jack had just finished working on this production, which was first screened in December 1975, by which time *Aces High* was in the can.

A few years earlier, Jack, a brilliant director and lovely man, had cast me in *Mad Jack* (1970), another thoughtful and highly acclaimed television film set in the First World War. This BBC Wednesday Play, by Tom Clarke, was about Siegfried Sassoon, played by Michael Jayston. I was cast as Ormand, his great friend. Studio filming was at Ealing Studios, home of the classic Ealing Comedies. But most of *Mad Jack* was filmed on location. At the audition I was asked if I could ride a horse. With foolhardy determination to get the role,

I replied yes. Riding a donkey on Bognor beach as a child was not the ideal preparation for what lay ahead in the countryside outside Weymouth. I had managed a couple of horse-riding lessons before my ordeal, but had hardly mastered trotting, let alone cantering or galloping. Now, on location, the owner of a local riding school proudly introduced me to a mighty beast called Paddy Punch. I was told he was quite old, very friendly, didn't get out much any more but really enjoyed a gallop when he had the chance. The scene involved riding towards Michael Jayston on his horse, coming from the other direction. We were to stop, have a conversation, then ride off in opposite directions. Michael, it turned out, was a very competent horseman. The inevitable happened. My horse refused to stop. We sped past Michael, with no time to talk. I clung on as we galloped into a wood, where at last we met a tree. Paddy Punch reared up and I slid off his back. Jack arrived and kindly asked if I was alright, then asked me to do it again. The same thing happened. We eventually managed to shoot the conversation by crew members holding the horses still. But it was no surprise when a couple of weeks later I was asked to go back to Weymouth to film the scene again. I hardly slept a wink in anticipation. We arrived at the location. To my surprise I could see no horses. Jack smiled, and told me to climb up on his shoulders. A member of the crew similarly lifted Michael on to his shoulders. We spoke our lines while jigged about by our two supporting gentlemen, who then turned and trotted away, with us as their jockeys. Remarkably, when I saw the film, this improvised activity looked remarkably convincing. I felt guilty, but was relieved and happy when the film won a major prize at the Monte Carlo Television Festival. By thus coming to my rescue, Jack had become a hero, and the chance to work with him again was irresistible.

It was a relief to know that no horses were to be involved in my *Aces High* scenes. Sitting on a saddle was replaced with sitting in the cockpit of one of the impressively restored SE5 biplanes that greeted us on our first day on location at Booker Airfield in

Buckinghamshire. Alongside the planes had been built a ruined house, in which Malcolm as Major Gresham had his office, and the wooden hut that served as the officers' mess.

It was a real pleasure to meet up with Malcolm again. We hadn't met since working together in *If....*, since when his rise to stardom had been meteoric and well-deserved. His appearances in Joseph Losey's *Figures in a Landscape* (1969) and in the principal role as Alex in Stanley Kubrick's controversial *A Clockwork Orange* (1971) had given him international recognition. I wondered if success had changed him. On our first day's shooting, before I had met up with him, it was announced that filming would be delayed for a few hours. A rumour went round that the reason for this was that Malcolm had arrived and discovered that a fridge, one of his contractual requirements, had not been installed in his caravan. Apparently he refused to work until this omission was rectified. Was this so-called starry behaviour? I never found out, but later that day we greeted each other like brothers, recalling our exciting and educational initiation into film acting, under the wise and unforgettable tuition of Lindsay Anderson. In fact, I felt that Malcolm had mellowed considerably since I witnessed his occasionally difficult behaviour on *If....* No temperament was on display. Perhaps this was partly due to the relaxed yet professional atmosphere on set that Jack Gold effortlessly engineered. Everybody was truly fond of him.

Parked at the edge of the airfield were the caravans in which we could change in and out of our uniforms and relax between takes. Jack asked if I wouldn't mind sharing mine with Peter Firth. As this was Peter's first film, and I was a decade older than him, Jack hoped I might look after him. Peter, it turned out, was a delightful caravan-mate, who needed no such support. He showed no nerves and his confident acting abilities were immediately apparent. In reality, he had had as much experience in front of the camera as I had, if not more, having been a child actor in several television series. On one memorable occasion he returned to the caravan and stood in the doorway with a perplexed frown. I asked him what was the matter. He shook his head. 'It's too easy,' he said, with no trace of showing off. He was worried, because he hadn't experienced any difficulty or doubt when acting his scene. It all came so naturally. A few weeks later I watched with admiration as he skilfully delivered a close-up. There were no words to say. The night before, his character had lost his virginity to a young French prostitute. He returned to the nightclub, his face radiant with excitement to meet her again, stopped as he entered, looked around and saw her. His excitement changed to surprise as he saw she was sitting with a German officer. She ignored Peter. His face crumpled. Summing up the situation he recovered his composure, then, bravely hiding his disappointment, turned and stoically departed. Every time I have since watched the film, that moment brings a lump to my throat. Pure magic. It was no surprise that Peter's next film, reprising his role in *Equus*, opposite Richard Burton, was so special. And his subsequent career has been consistently impressive.

I loved working on *Aces High*. It never felt like work. Early each day I drove up the M4 to Booker, near High Wycombe, enjoyed the company of the cast and crew, indulged in delicious bacon butties for breakfast, and shared lunch with Peter in the caravan, sometimes joined by Malcolm or Simon, passing the time swapping stories. Jack's direction was clear and helpful. I can remember no tension or tantrums on set. And I remember with gratitude one kind gesture made by Derek Cracknell, the efficient yet thoughtful Assistant Director. My status in the actors' hierarchy wasn't high enough to warrant a stand-in. After rehearsing a scene, actors with star status would retire to their caravans while stand-ins took their place on set and the lighting was arranged. Derek noticed that this meant that my regular conversations with Malcolm were often interrupted. To my amazement he arranged for me to have a stand-in. Feeling a little guilty, I happily accepted this perk.

I grew to love my character Tommy. Alongside his extrovert bonhomie and ever-optimistic attitude, lay a serious belief in the importance of fastidiously checking his equipment. The scene in which I earnestly explained to young Croft my belief in CMD – Confidence in Mechanical Details – was a joy to play. As was the scene in which I could display an over-the-top ebullience as we young officers lapped up an enticing slideshow of semi-naked ladies in saucy postcard poses. Jack encouraged me to smoke a cigar and improvise hand shadow animals on the screen and make appropriately licentious comments. I remember licking my lips at an exotic scene with a topless girl surrounded by wild animals. 'Give me the lion's share anytime!' I smirked.

In such scenes of drink-fuelled frivolity in the mess, Jack gave us a remarkably free rein to enjoy ourselves. When Malcolm, as Gresham, delivered us the German officer he had captured, we gave him a right royal welcome, wearing improvised fancy dress, banging kitchen utensils, and ending up with a free-for-all pillow fight. Jack imposed very little choreography on the action, allowing us to enjoy the mock fight with energetic abandon. The scene illustrated how important it must have been for young officers like this, in wartime mortal danger, knowing their life expectancy was so limited, to be given the chance to let their hair down like naughty schoolboys.

The film also showed how they relaxed, by playing snooker or by making their own entertainment. There was an upright piano in the mess, and I had a ball singing a couple of songs from the period, egged on by my tipsy comrades, laughing and joining in the grizzly words. Making light of the horror was the best way to cope.

As the bold aviator was dying
And as 'neath the wreckage he lay
To the sobbing mechanics about him
These last parting words he did say...

Take the cylinders out of my kidneys
The connecting rod out of my brain
From the small of my back get the crankshaft
And assemble the engine again!

'It's the Only, Only Way' was another ironically jolly ditty I sang, dancing my way out of the mess with a flourish. Tommy's uninhibited clowning gave me an opportunity to show off, and I thoroughly enjoyed it.

Playing the piano in this scene was Christopher Plummer as 'Uncle' Sinclair. In fact he was miming to recorded accompaniment. But he later took us by surprise by beautifully playing, for real, during our aforementioned pillow fight. His delicate rendition of a classical music theme provided a delicious counterpoint to our rumbustious free-for-all. I later read that Christopher was a trained musician, who could have become a concert pianist. The quiet unassuming manner in which he offered to play during the scene was typical of this softly spoken, civilised actor whose career had encompassed leading Shakespearean roles. On a school party visit, I had been privileged to see him play Henry II in Jean Anouilh's *Becket* at the Aldwych Theatre (1961). He was a true Hollywood star, without all the accompanying razzmatazz, a friendly and cooperative team member.

Shooting at locations other than Booker Airfield were for me few but great fun. One memorable location shoot was for a scene where a group of us officers piled into a handsome vintage car, and set off for a boozy night on the town. Locations had been found in London to masquerade as the French town Rouen. Simon drove, with Malcolm sitting beside him, and Peter and I squashed together in the back with Elliot Cooper and Christopher Blake playing Wade and Roberts. For our arrival, we took over a corner of Covent Garden, and, after midnight, Simon drove us under the portico of St Paul's Church. We rowdily set off for the entrance to a nightclub, using a narrow alleyway off Garrick Street or Bedford Street as the club's exterior. It felt intoxicating to be given licence to behave outrageously in the West End, and this was before we indulged in too much alcohol – not for real, of course – in the smoke-filled basement club. We shot this interior scene on another day, somewhere in St Katharine Docks, in impressive cellars with bricked pillars and alcoves. Jeanne Patou, the French chanteuse, provided appropriate songs, accompanied by recordings of a band featuring an accordion. A team of extras provided atmosphere. Before shooting started, Jack explained what he wanted us to do, encouraging us to be loud and extroverted. I pointed out to him a particularly beautiful young lady, sitting with other actresses waiting to perform. Jack smiled, and minutes later the young lady was sitting on my lap! She joined in the uninhibited scene with enthusiasm. Judy Buxton later played major classical roles for the Royal Shakespeare Company, and appeared regularly on television. Many years later we were reunited in Eastbourne, where I was visiting my touring theatre company and she was appearing in a play with her husband Jeffrey Holland, star of the popular *Hi-de-Hi!* television series. Jack gave us all fairly free rein to improvise around the dialogue, and most of our laughter was totally genuine. At one point, Peter, as young Croft, was leaving the table on his way to losing his virginity. As he stood up, a hook on his belt got caught on his chair, causing it to drag along the floor. We all roared. And Jack kept this unplanned moment in the final cut.

When I first saw *Aces High* I couldn't but help be impressed, as were the critics, by the specially filmed aerial battle sequences. But we actors, of course, were never permitted, let alone able, to fly our SE5s. We were occasionally allowed to jump into our cockpits or watch as the propellers were activated. It was a sobering thought that our real counterparts were not allowed to use parachutes if in dire peril. Close-ups on our faces as we flew were necessary, so a mock-up section of aircraft was raised on supports above the ground, and one by one we filmed our actions and reactions in side view and through the cockpit screen. For each take, Jack called up his instructions from the ground below, and wind and smoke machines were turned on as appropriate. For me, this involved smiling to Croft in the plane alongside, concentrating hard through my goggles, and occasionally waving to my comrades after a successful manoeuvre. When Tommy's plane is hit, it bursts into flames, and it was necessary to see my face gradually burn and blacken as the fire took hold. The make-up department carefully applied a charcoal-like substance, increasing its intensity for each progressive take. Flames were aimed at me from long tubes resembling scaffolding poles. They blasted into and past the windscreen, as I appeared to dodge them. During this process, my forehead, exposed above my goggles, was inadvertently singed, and I needed to apply a soothing cream to it for a couple of days. Nothing serious compared to what was happening to Tommy, but it reminded me of what those real young pilots had to face.

In the film, my character is seen engulfed in flames, climbing from his cockpit and jumping to his death on the ground below. I'm glad to say that a courageous stunt man acted as my double for this sequence. I watched as he was set alight and, on 'Action', jumped onto the carefully prepared cardboard boxes that were to break his fall. My heart skipped a beat as he landed and rolled over, knocking down the man poised with a fire extinguisher to squirt him and put out the fire. Luckily a second fireman was standing by prepared for such an eventuality. The flames were extinguished and all was well.

In recent years, *Aces High* has been regularly screened on television, usually in a daytime slot. This has meant, to my frustration, that my dramatic death scene, and also my favourite scene in which we ogle at naughty pictures in the slideshow, have been censored, cut completely because presumably they are too sensational for the stomachs of the teatime audience. I think Jack, who sadly died in 2015, would be saddened as much as me by such vandalism!

A few months after filming, news came through that we were to have a Royal premiere, at the ABC 1, Shaftesbury Avenue, in aid of the Soldiers, Sailors, Airmen and Family Association. Needing to wear evening dress for the occasion, I decided to push the boat out and visit the legendary Douglas Hayward, tailor to the stars. In his salon in Mount Street, looked down on by photos of Mr Hayward's clients, including Michael Caine, Peter Sellers, Terence Stamp and a host of other luminaries, I waited for my first fitting along with the racing driver Jackie Stewart. My specially designed suit included a trendy dark blue velvet jacket. It cost an arm and a leg (no pun intended), but I felt, as I stood in the line-up to meet the royal party, that it was worth every penny. I stood between Simon Ward and Richard Johnson, as Her Majesty the Queen came down the line. She asked me if we had actually flown the aeroplanes. I replied that insurance wouldn't have allowed that, then followed her magnetic gaze as she moved on. A sudden dig in the ribs from Richard Johnson swung my head back to find the Duke of Edinburgh patiently waiting to shake my hand. He was followed by Earl Mountbatten.

The Royal premiere of *Aces High* coincided with another celebration. Four days earlier Jacqui, my wife, had given birth to our first child, Katherine. She was still in hospital, but the consultant gave her special permission to attend the premiere as long as she was back in the ward by midnight. She had already prepared her outfit. I delivered it to the hospital in the morning, and we had a *Daily Express* photo-call with the new baby. In the early evening a car delivered us to the cinema, outside which more photographs were taken. While I stood in the line-up to meet Her Majesty, Jacqui joined others in a cordoned-off area, where she met Prince Philip. After the film, Cinderella-like, she was driven back to the hospital. Next morning, we discovered that we were front-page news, becoming the main subject of the premiere's publicity coverage. I hope the film producers and Malcolm didn't feel we had stolen their thunder.

I must admit that *Aces High* could have given me a taste for Hollywood-style stardom. I was asked to represent the film at a charity showing in a cinema near Clapham Junction. I dressed up in my Dougie Hayward suit, and a limousine took me to the cinema, where I was greeted by the charity's representative. He apologised profusely that there had been a major hiccup with the invitations. As a result, there were only a handful of supporters sitting in the Stalls and I sat with the embarrassed organisers and the cinema manager in an otherwise empty Circle. Perhaps this was an amusing omen, trying to tell me that celebrity stardom was not really my thing. But I did also represent *Aces High* at the Cork Film Festival, where I was royally entertained and taken to kiss the Blarney Stone. My sense of humour, however, was again triggered – the cinema across the square was clearly visible from the hotel, yet another limo grandly drove me the couple of hundred yards to where the local dignitaries were waiting.

Newspaper reviews were positive if not ecstatic. In *The Times*, Philip French wrote, '*Aces High* may not be as good as Gold's best television work, but it's his most successful movie since his auspicious feature film debut with *The Bofors Gun*.' He praised the fact that:

> (Howard) Barker and his director Jack Gold have not set out to mock these potentially ludicrous Western Front heroes but rather to re-create their world and to convey what it was that made them endure day after day in the knowledge that they were doomed to almost certain death and that the war in which they were engaged was an exercise in futility.

In the *Sunday Telegraph*, Tom Hutchinson said the film 'deserves sky-high praise.' Tom Milne in the *Observer* disagreed:

> Not content with drenching the whole film in nostalgic songs in imitation of 'Oh! What a Lovely War', scriptwriter Howard Barker

and director Jack Gold have also coarsened every situation in the play (Journey's End), added a number of hoary clichés (including a first romantic disillusionment for the boy about to die) and turned its movingly understated message into a shrill anti-Establishment squawk.

Derek Malcolm in the *Guardian* was particularly generous to the actors:

Peter Firth's new boy at the flying field is a particularly fresh and intense performance; Malcolm McDowell as the leader of the pack, his former house-captain, and Simon Ward, the cad in the throes of a nervous breakdown, are also strong and resourceful. Christopher Plummer and David Wood as the squadron's two most human members have seldom been better on-screen, and there are good cameos from Trevor Howard, Richard Johnson and Ray Milland, guzzling lunch and digesting Cabinet gossip at Brigade HQ. It's a cast without a serious flaw and a film which credibly echoes a past that, quite incredibly, belongs to our own century.

General opinion, as the decades have passed, seems to be one of approval, and it is pleasing that *Aces High* has so regularly been screened on the major television channels. Its anti-war message seems to me to be still extremely relevant.

Many of my fellow actors in *Aces High* are sadly no longer with us. Simon Ward worked regularly in stage, film and television, notably as Sir Monty Everard in the BBC series *Judge John Deed*, until his death in 2012.

Richard Johnson's versatile career continued until his death in 2015. He co-starred as Dr Watson opposite Charlton Heston's Sherlock Holmes in *The Crucifer of Blood* (1991) and, having played many roles for the Royal Shakespeare Company in the 1970s, including Antony opposite Janet Suzman's Cleopatra, returned to

Stratford in 1992 in *All's Well that Ends Well*. One of his last film appearances was in *The Boy in the Striped Pyjamas* (2008). He died in 2015.

Christopher Plummer worked solidly and successfully until his death in 2021 at the age of ninety-one. He won the Oscar for Best Supporting Actor at the age of eighty-two for *Beginners* (2010) and became the oldest actor ever to be nominated for an Oscar at the age of eighty-eight for *All the Money in the World*.

After winning the BAFTA for Best Actor in television's *The Jewel in the Crown* (1985), Tim Pigott-Smith achieved fame in films, including *Gangs of New York* (2002) and *Quantum of Solace* (2008) and onstage in *King Charles III* (2014), for which he was nominated for Olivier and Tony Awards, and as a notable King Lear at the West Yorkshire Playhouse (2011). He died, aged seventy, in 2017.

Sitting cross-legged in the publicity team photo was the closest I came to working with the legends Ray Milland and Trevor Howard, who died in 1986 and 1988 respectively. I wish I could have observed them on set, but we had no scenes together.

I last met my favourite director, Jack Gold, at a conference about children's television in the early 2000s. In 1998 he had directed a highly praised television adaptation of Michelle Magorian's award-winning novel *Goodnight Mister Tom*, starring John Thaw. We shared a deep admiration for the book, and when my stage adaptation won an Olivier Award in 2013, Jack was kind enough to send congratulations. He died two years later, and is much missed.

Peter Firth is happily still with us, perhaps best known for his role as Sir Harry Pearce in the BBC's *Spooks*. He is the only actor to have appeared in every episode of the show's ten series. On film he played in *The Hunt for Red October* (1990) and *Amistad* (1997).

Malcolm McDowell has for many years lived in California and worked mainly in the United States. In April 2019 it was a real pleasure to be reunited, when Malcolm came to London to

Party is over for Cinders on the stroke of midnight

Jacqueline at last night's premiere

Pictures by
Hilaria McCarthy

ACTRESS Jacqueline Stanburg was the Cinderella of a royal film premiere last night.

Before the clock struck 12 she kept her word and slipped quietly away from the glittering West End occasion.

But it was not because her clothes would turn to rags.

The reason was that her four-day-old daughter, Katherine, was waiting to be fed at Queen Mary's Hospital, Roehampton, Surrey.

The hospital allowed the beautiful actress to visit the cinema to see her husband, actor David Wood, being presented to the Queen.

Exciting

But they insisted that she be back in the hospital by midnight.

"Hungry babies don't wait for anyone," said Jacqueline before leaving for the Shaftesbury Avenue screening of "Aces High," co-starring her husband.

"Katherine is our first baby and we are both over the moon.

"It has really been an exciting few days for David. Seeing his daughter one day and meeting the Queen the next.

"I just couldn't have stayed in hospital while David was having his big day outside."

Ian Christie reviews
The film, Page 11

Cinderella . . . Jacqueline Stanburg with her husband and daughter

Aces High: *The 'Cinderella' newspaper story – baby Katherine, Jacqui and me.*

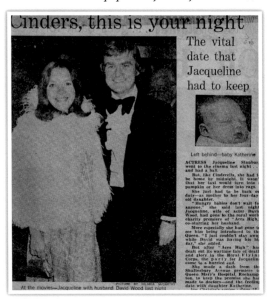

Cinders, this is your night

The vital date that Jacqueline had to keep

Left behind—baby Katherine

ACTRESS Jacqueline Stanburg went to the cinema last night . . . and had a ball.

But, like Cinderella, she had to be home by midnight. It wasn't that her taxi would turn into a pumpkin or her dress into rags.

She just had to be back on duty—as mother to her four-day-old daughter.

"Hungry babies don't wait for anyone," she said last night. Jacqueline, wife of actor David Wood, had gone to the royal world charity premiere of "Aces High," co-starring her husband.

More especially she had gone to see him being introduced to the Queen. "I just couldn't stay away while David was having his big day," she added.

But after "Aces High" had dealt out its wartime tale of death and glory in the Royal Flying Corps, the party for Jacqueline came to a hurried end.

She made a dash from the Shaftesbury Avenue premiere to Queen Mary's Hospital, Roehampton, to keep the promise she had made to doctors . . . and the feeding date with daughter Katherine.

Ian Christie's review . . . Page 13

At the movies—Jacqueline with husband, David Wood, last night

PICTURE BY HILARIA McCARTHY

Aces High: *The 'Cinderella' newspaper story –*
Jacqui and me at the Royal Première.

Reunited with Malcolm McDowell, fifty years after If.... *and forty-three years after* Aces High.

North Sea Hijack: *Newspaper advertisement.*

North Sea Hijack: *Me with Anthony Perkins.*

North Sea Hijack: *My close-up masterclass.*
L to R – Me, James Mason, Anthony Perkins,
Roger Moore (back to camera).

Poster advertising my play, The Plotters
of Cabbage Patch Corner.

Back Home: *The team photo. Piers Haggard (director) sits with the two Hayleys. I'm on the left in the pink trousers, next to co-producer Nigel Pickard.*

Back Home: *The two Hayleys, Carr and Mills.*

EIIR

The Master of the Household

has received Her Majesty's command to invite

Mrs. Jacqueline Wood

to a Party to celebrate British Children's Literature

in the Garden of Buckingham Palace

on Sunday, 25th June, 2006

In Confirmation   *This card does not admit*

Please see the enclosed information about access and conditions of entry to Buckingham Palace.

Bringing children's literature to life at Buckingham Palace

The Children's Party at the Palace: My wife
Jacqui's ticket, and the folder it came in.

The Cast
In order of appearance

Huw Edwards....................................*Newsreader*	Kacey Ainsworth................................*Peter Pan*
Sophie Raworth.......................................*Reporter*	Kelly Osbourne..*Wendy*
Meera Syal..............................*Mary The Maid*	Sanjeev Bhaskar............................*Robin Hood*
Ronnie Corbett.......................................*Mr Tibbs*	Sam Aston.................................*Horrid Henry*
Gavin Lee.............*Bert the Chimney Sweep*	Luke Tittensor ....*Just William*
Sophie Dahl......................................*Sophie Dahl*	Janine Duvitski..................*Martha The Maid*
Jonathan Ross..........................*Fat Controller*	Oliver Symons..................*Mrs Tiggy-Winkle*
Bradley Walsh.................................*Burglar Bill*	Antoinette Brooks-Daw........*Angelina Ballerina*
Patsy Kensit.......................*Grand High Witch*	Martin Clunes.......................................*Mr Plod*
Anthony Head...............................*Captain Hook*	Harry Hill.......................................*Owl Keeper*
June Brown......................................*Aunt Spiker*	Zoe Salmon...................*Famous Five – George*
Pam St Clement..........................*Aunt Sponge*	Gethin Jones.....................*Famous Five – Dick*
Richard O'Brien...........................*Childcatcher*	Konnie Huq....................*Famous Five – Anne*
Amanda Redman.......................*Cruella De Vil*	Matt Baker.......................*Famous Five – Julian*
Nicholas Lyndhurst..............*Cruella's Chauffeur*	Mabel the dog.................*Famous Five – Timmy*
Joe Pasquale.................................*White Rabbit*	*the dog*
Dani Harmer...................................*Tracy Beaker*	Alan Titchmarsh.............*Percy the Park Keeper*
Darragh Mortell...*Crash*	Fiona Bruce...................*Crimewatch Presenter*
Montanna Thompson...............................*Justine*	Nick Ross.....................*Crimewatch Presenter*
Matt Stevens..*Busker*	Daniel Radcliffe.......................*Harry Potter*
Bernard Cribbins....................*Ticket Inspector*	Rupert Grint................................*Ron Weasley*
Rani Khanijau..*Badger*	Emma Watson..................*Hermoine Granger*
Lizzie Greenwood-Hughes...........................*Mole*	Matthew Lewis.................*Neville Longbottom*
Lizo Mzimba..*Toad*	Scarlett Strallen..........................*Mary Poppins*
Simon Grant...*Owl*	Amanda Symonds............................*Mrs Corry*
Anne Foy...*Pussycat*	Georgia Russell..................................*Jane Banks*
Tony Hasnath...*Mowgli*	Lawrence Michalowski.................*Michael Banks*
Jerry Hall.........................*Queen Of The Pirates*	

The Band of the Welsh Guards

Director of Music Major David Cresswell BBCM psm, appears by permission of
Colonel A J E Malcolm OBE, The Regimental Lieutenant Colonel

The Queen's Handbag: *The cast list.*

*The Children's Party at the Palace: The stage and
audience in Buckingham Palace Gardens.*

The Queen's Handbag: *The Queen, reunited with her handbag, is pleased to find her speech.*

The Queen's Handbag: *Tracy Beaker returns the handbag to the Queen. L to R – Her Majesty, Prince Philip, Dani Harmer, Martin Clunes, Ronnie Corbett, June Brown, Joe Pasquale, Gavin Lee, Patsy Kensit, Sophie Dahl, Alan Titchmarsh.*

celebrate the fiftieth anniversary of *A Clockwork Orange*. We had a nostalgic catch-up over a cream tea at the Dorchester Hotel. I look back on our work together in Lindsay Anderson's *If....* and Jack Gold's *Aces High* with pride and pleasure.

LESS IS MOORE

1979

North Sea Hijack starring Roger Moore, Anthony Perkins and James Mason

It was surreal. There I was in Galway, at 3am – three o'clock in the morning! – sitting at a cramped table in an oil rig supply vessel chatting with three iconic screen characters, James Bond, Norman Bates (Psycho) and Humbert Humbert (Lolita) – in person, Roger Moore, Anthony Perkins and James Mason – and I was about to shoot a scene and share the silver screen with them...

In April 1979 I was asked to audition for a film called *Esther, Ruth and Jennifer*. At Pinewood I met the director, an American giant called Andrew V. McLaglen, well known for his action films featuring stars like John Wayne, James Stewart and Richard Burton. I cannot remember being asked to read anything, but I was asked if I could do a Scottish accent. Remembering my Theatre In Education experience in *The Tay Bridge Disaster*, I reckoned I could get away with it. I was offered the role of Herring, a newspaper reporter who arranges for an American group of journalists to board an oil rig supply vessel, servicing an oil rig in the North Sea. The journalists, played by Anthony Perkins of *Psycho* fame, and Michael Parks, turn out to be baddies, who take over the ship and demand a huge ransom from the British government, headed by a woman Prime Minister (several years before Mrs Thatcher arrived in the post), in exchange for not blowing up the oil rig.

The hero of this action movie was played by Roger Moore, who had filmed *The Wild Geese* with Richard Burton for the same director the previous year. James Mason played an Admiral, caught up in the ensuing negotiations.

Accepting the role made me feel somewhat guilty, because Jacqui was pregnant with our second child, and filming was due to take place in Galway, Ireland. Jacqui generously agreed to let me go, and, only a week or so after the audition, I set off.

Galway is a beautiful place, but I didn't see much of it, because most days we were on a real oil rig supply vessel from very early in the morning through to 6pm in the evening, often looking for bad weather! Several scenes demanded a tempestuous sea, so most of the cast had to be on board each day, whether or not they were in scenes scheduled for that day. Most of the time we huddled in the ship's crew room. Quite where the real Norwegian crew relaxed, I don't know. Fears of seasickness were partly allayed by the presence of a nurse with a large supply of pills. I remember the lovely American-Irish actor Philip O'Brien plotting to divert the nurse from her medical kit in order to steal extra pills. In the event, the only seasickness sufferer was a tough-looking prop man, who only lasted one day at sea. Some of us wondered whether it was a cunning ploy to have a few days off.

Much of my time in the crew room was spent with Anthony Perkins, who was extremely friendly and very accomplished at word games, many of which he apparently played with Stephen Sondheim back home. He came up with some ingenious anagrams, of which my favourite was 'ROAST MULES'. Several of us spent days trying to work it out! The letters form just one word…

When we first arrived in Galway, those of us playing the smaller roles were directed to several caravans used as dressing rooms, alongside the make-up and wardrobe departments and catering wagon. Several of us sat chatting when we heard Roger Moore arriving and being led to his trailer. He was shown our caravan and popped his head round the door. 'Ah, the act-ors!' he loudly exclaimed. This was the first example of his self-deprecatory humour, which was noticeable throughout filming. He always decried his own acting ability, and also delightfully joked with crew and cast, as though he was being paid a considerable salary simply to entertain everybody. He never appeared to display ill-humour or artistic temperament. Everybody loved him.

The hotel most of us stayed in wasn't grand, but was comfortable, apart from the couple of occasions when it became the subject of an IRA bomb scare, which meant we all had to evacuate the premises for several hours until the police had done a thorough check. The radio by the side of my bed had an aggravating habit of never turning completely off. Faint music could be heard from the speaker both day and night. No one at reception seemed able to cure the problem, and for some reason there was no plug or switch with which to turn it off. Most nights, having returned from our adventures at sea, I was too tired to notice. Also, I never got over the effect of being at sea for so long each day. Returning to the hotel, walking along the corridor felt like swaying from side to side on a tossing ship.

My first day of shooting was on terra firma. I was driven along the quayside with Mr Perkins and Mr Parks, then welcomed aboard by Jack Watson, who was playing the ship's captain. My first lines had to be shouted from the quay to Mr Watson on the bridge. To my embarrassment, the authenticity of my Scottish accent was immediately questioned by Mr McLaglen, the director. Hopefully I managed to improve it. The fact that an American had questioned its accuracy made the reprimand even more galling.

My scenes on board were fun, even though, once the ship had been hijacked, the ship's crew suspected me of being one of the baddies, and roughed me up before gagging me and shutting me in a cupboard. All in the line of duty.

In fact I received a bit of a shock when, halfway through filming, Mr McLaglen asked to see me. He told me that the powers that be had decided that I was really a baddie. There had been no indication of this in the script, and I certainly had thought that I was an innocent reporter who became unwittingly embroiled in the plot. But no, I was apparently complicit in the hijack. This made me think back on all the previous scenes. Should I have acted the baddie? Mr McLaglen said that it didn't make the slightest bit of difference. He just wanted me to know. Somewhat bemused, I carried on.

In week four of filming we did a night shoot. The ship was docked for the scene in which a helicopter lands Roger Moore,

James Mason and David Hedison on the deck, in order to satisfy the demands of Mr Perkins, with the intention of guaranteeing the ransom. I found myself sharing a table in the crew room with James Mason, Anthony Perkins and Roger Moore. It seemed quite surreal, but conversation was friendly, even though it was about 3am in the morning.

Mr McLaglen had asked if I could wear my own glasses. These were round, wire-framed, with blue lenses. I've no idea why I chose to wear these in my private life. I suppose I must have thought them trendy. Shortly before shooting, one of the tiny screws fell out, releasing one of the lenses. This caused a slight panic, because I didn't have a spare pair. It had already been noted that my stunt double, who had to be shot from a height and tumble to the deck, would need to wear my glasses. And I needed them in the scene leading up to my shooting. It was quite dark in the crew room, but I was impressed, and even charmed, when Roger Moore joined me scrabbling around on the floor to find the missing screw. And, when eventually it was found, he helped me carefully screw it back into place, using fingernails as a substitute screwdriver.

Shooting the scene taught me a big lesson about film acting. Mr McLaglen held up a long stick. The top of it, he told us, indicated the motion of the approaching helicopter. In individual close-ups, Messrs Moore, Perkins, Mason and I were to follow the progress of the helicopter through the night sky. Being the junior member of the cast, my close-up was first. Acting my socks off, or rather acting my eyes off, I furrowed my brow slightly, peered upwards at the stick, wondering first if it was indeed the helicopter, then deciding that it was, then widening my eyes as Mr McLaglen lowered the stick. Mr Mason came next. It was noticeable that his expression hardly changed throughout the take. A slight frown, perhaps. Mr Perkins appeared to do absolutely nothing whatsoever with his eyes or face. Finally, Mr Moore raised one characteristically quizzical eyebrow. The lesson I learned was that film acting demanded much less rather than more. When your face is filling the screen, better to just think than try to emote. In the final film, of course, the three stars seem to be reacting perfectly in character to the arrival of the helicopter, whereas I look a bit like an animated puppet.

In the UK, the film was released in 1980 as *North Sea Hijack*. It didn't set the world on fire, but it is regularly repeated on television and was, for me, an eye-opening encounter with the world of Hollywood, albeit shot in Galway. I never met or worked again with anyone involved with the film, and many are sadly no longer with us.

The answer to Mr Perkins's anagram is 'SOMERSAULT'.

DISNEY DEALINGS

1972–2006

Featuring *Back Home* starring Hayley Mills

The opportunity to work for Disney as an actor never presented itself. But, having discovered an outstanding children's novel, I became passionately determined to adapt it for television. I had no idea that the labour of love that followed would lead me along an unconventional route to becoming a Disney-approved writer and the recipient of a Daytime Emmy nomination.

In the 1960s Disney released a considerable number of family films. Considering how important family entertainment became in my subsequent writing career, it is surprising how few of them I saw. I remember being moved by the story of *Greyfriars Bobby*, and I was certainly impressed by the brilliant, animated version of *One Hundred and One Dalmatians*. Disney's gift was, and is, to make the young audience care. A strong sense of justice prevails, an ingredient I have found extremely useful in my plays. Children know all about fairness and unfairness. 'It's not fair' is one of the first things they learn to say. If one child sees another receive two pieces of chocolate when he or she has only been given one, feelings run high. And Disney's craft in storytelling has always been impeccable, ensuring the young viewer is eager to know what comes next, and employing plots and characters with just enough of a melodramatic quality to grab their emotions.

I was excited when, in the early 1970s, Eva Redfern, Disney's representative in London, asked to meet me, scouting for talent to recommend to her bosses in Hollywood. She took me to lunch and told me she had enjoyed seeing a performance of my children's play *The Plotters of Cabbage Patch Corner* during its Christmas season in 1972 at the Shaw Theatre in London. This was my first original play, following two adaptations. Set in a garden, the story involved a conflict between the pretty insects and the ugly insects. The garden was owned by the Big Ones, unseen human beings whose booming voices were heard as they sprayed the ugly insects with anti-insect spray. In retaliation the Uglies went on strike, and the Pretties fought against them in order to save their home. I suppose it was a 'green' play, written some years before green issues rightly became fashionable. The play had received some encouraging reviews, and Eva said that Disney might be interested in creating an animated version. I was naturally flattered, and imagined my story, characters and the songs for which I had written both music and lyrics, being translated to the big screen. But as our discussion progressed, I think Eva began to see how passionate I was about providing entertainment of integrity for children, and sensed how proprietorial I felt about my work. She explained that Disney might be willing to pay a considerable sum for my *Plotters* property, but that once I had signed the contract, I would probably no longer be involved. My story would be developed by an experienced team of writers. New songs would be written and composed by Disney songwriters, and I would have to accept that the end product might have little resemblance to my original creation. Eva eventually, I think, understood when I said I felt unable to accept such a proposal. We said goodbye. I thanked her for her interest and honesty, and that was the end of it.

Fifteen years passed before Disney featured once more in my working life. I found myself working with the Disney Channel, which specialised in family dramas made for television. This association, not initiated by me, led to my most successful partnership with Disney. By this time I was co-director with Maureen Harter of a small television production company. The monopoly of the big television companies had been broken. Independents were now allowed to pitch and create programmes for the mainstream channels. Maureen and I had produced for Channel 4 their first ever children's series called *Chips' Comic*. Channel 4 at that time had no children's department, so we approached the Education Department and successfully pitched for a series aimed at children with learning difficulties. We started looking for other projects.

In 1985 we began a long quest to co-produce a full-length family film. This was *Back Home*, adapted from Michelle Magorian's outstanding book, which I discovered when I was a judge of the Whitbread Children's Book Award. It was the one book I couldn't put down. Telling a tale of a young girl evacuated to America in the Second World War and the difficulty she faced on her return to England when hostilities ceased, I knew it had all the ingredients for a film or television adaptation. Our company, Verronmead Ltd., managed to get the rights and, realising that we were too small an outfit to achieve production on our own, we searched for a more prestigious co-producer. We were lucky to find a champion in Nigel Pickard, a producer at Southern Television. While he searched for the finance, I embarked upon a screenplay. We were elated when Nigel told us that the Disney Channel was interested, partly because when Rusty, the girl in the story, comes home, she has become Americanised. This suggested that she would best be played by a young American actress. Our delight was somewhat tempered by the fact that the Disney people enthusiastically announced that they would find a suitable screenplay writer. Nigel diplomatically told them that a British writer had already started work, and they agreed to wait to see a first draft. Although I had by then finished writing, we decided to wait three months before sending my efforts to Disney, reckoning that if we were to send the script too soon, we might be thought to be presenting them with a fait accompli. The plan succeeded. My screenplay was accepted, and finance was agreed. The highly respected director Piers Haggard came on board. I had last worked with him as an actor in *The Love School*, a BBC classic series about the Pre-Raphaelites. We were thrilled when Hayley Mills agreed to play Rusty's mother.

Exactly how we managed to secure Hayley Mills's services I don't know. Did the Disney Channel suggest her? She was now in her forties, but her many leading roles for Disney, as a child and a teenager, still identified her as a Disney star. *Pollyanna* (1960) and *The Parent Trap* (1961) are still Disney classics. For me, even more memorable were her non-Disney roles in *Tiger Bay* (1959) and *Whistle Down the Wind* (1961). Maybe Piers, our director, thought of her for *Back Home*. However it came about, her casting as Peggy Dickinson was perfect. The mature Hayley played Peggy with a sympathetic spirit of resilience coping with the problems endured by many young mothers whose husbands went off to fight in the Second World War. She portrayed beautifully the transition of a stay-at-home wife to a stalwart WVS worker, acquiring vehicle maintenance skills.

I remember much admiring Hayley's bravura performance onstage as Peter Pan in 1969. Since seeing the play several times as a child, the play had a considerable influence on my eventual writing career as a children's playwright. I collect Peter Pans, having seen Margaret Lockwood and her daughter Julia play the role, as well as Joan Greenwood, Janette Scott, Susannah York and Dorothy Tutin. Hayley was up there with the very best, conveying not just the adventurousness of the character, but also the eventual heartlessness. And this was Hayley's first professional stage appearance. Furthermore, her achievement was the greater because, for the first time in many years, the venue had changed from the comparatively intimate auditorium of the Scala Theatre to the wide open spaces of the New Victoria Cinema. In 2004, as Chair of the organisation Action for Children's Arts, I arranged and hosted the centenary of *Peter Pan* at the Duke of York's Theatre, where J.M. Barrie's masterpiece had first been produced. Many incumbents of the roles of Peter Pan and Captain Hook came and shared memories of their performances. They included Wendy Craig, Susannah York, Janette Scott, Donald Sinden, Ron Moody and John McCallum. And, to my delight, Hayley flew especially from New York to take part.

I had first met her in 1978, when her then partner, Leigh Lawson, played the lead in *The Luck of the Bodkins*, the P.G. Wodehouse adaptation I had co-written with John Gould. We played a season at the Theatre Royal, Windsor, and occasionally Hayley would meet us for tea after rehearsal. She was always friendly, interested and supportive. Now, eleven years later, I was thrilled to actually be working with her.

Audition tapes for Rusty were arranged in America, and another Hayley, Hayley Carr, was cast. By coincidence, she had been named after Hayley Mills, who was a great favourite of young Hayley's mother. For Grandmother, I suggested the wonderful Jean Anderson, with whom I had acted in another BBC classic serial, Turgenev's *Fathers and Sons*. Jean agreed to play the part, and was joined by Brenda Bruce and Rupert Frazer. Filming began and for me it was a very exciting time. The whole production team were superb, and watching them work on location was a treat. Only once did I step out of line by talking to an actor about his character. Piers was rightly cross with me. Any advice or thoughts should always go through the director.

The two Hayleys worked beautifully together and I often wondered whether the elder Hayley, working alongside the younger Hayley, who was eleven years old, was reminded of her own early days in front of the camera. She certainly was an excellent role model, patient and positive, caring and helpful. The younger Hayley must have gained confidence from observing the professionalism of the elder Hayley. Their mother and daughter relationship on screen was very real and moving.

I think we did justice to Michelle's classic story. Winning a Gold Award at the New York Film & TV Festival in 1991 was the icing on the cake. And I was nominated for a Daytime Emmy for the screenplay. ITV chose to screen the play at 9pm during the summer. The reviews were mixed. The critics who gave us lukewarm reviews had perhaps assumed that, in such a prime-time slot, they would be watching an adult film rather than a family piece. The production was never repeated or released on video in the UK. In America, however, it was shown many times over the years on the Disney Channel and appeared on video. Verronmead was very proud to be the instigating partner, and I became a Disney-approved writer.

Verronmead proposed an adaptation of *The Flawed Glass*, a moving and heart-warming story by Ian Strachan. Set on a remote island off the coast of Scotland, the heroine Shona Macleod, barely able to walk and speak, is isolated by her disabilities. When a wealthy American businessman buys the island and moves his family there, Shona forges a remarkable friendship with his son. To our disappointment, the Disney Channel turned this down. Fortunately, attitudes regarding the portrayal of disability on-screen have advanced considerably, to the extent that compelling stories have been adapted successfully for a receptive audience. But sadly the opportunity never arose to write for Disney again.

My next brush with Disney came out of the blue. In 2000, I was on holiday with my family in Cornwall when I received a phone call from Los Angeles. Somehow the caller, Mireya Hepner, had managed to obtain my mother-in-law's number. Mireya, or Murry, as I was later allowed to call her, was ringing from Disney. Having spent many years as a stage manager, including touring with the legendary Marcel Marceau, she had been employed by Disney to improve the quality of their arena shows. Murry had trained in London at LAMDA and, for the Christmas season 1977 she had worked as an usher at the Old Vic, where my children's musical *The Gingerbread Man* was playing. Murry said she watched the show about forty times and was impressed by the way it entertained the children. She wanted to see if I would be interested in working on a project for Disney. I said yes, and we agreed to meet several weeks later in Oxford, where my adaptation of *Spot's Birthday Party* would be playing at the Playhouse. Before the meeting my agent advised me that Disney would expect me to sign a contract that would assign to them anything I said, even in this preliminary meeting. I warily agreed, but when I met Murry, whom I immediately liked,

I said I would be saying very little and not revealing too many of my ideas. Not that I had any at that stage. It wasn't until the Oxford meeting that I was told that the project involved *Winnie-the-Pooh*. Disney, who had acquired the full rights to the famous British bear in March 2001 for $350 million, were planning a big arena version, and Murry wanted me to craft the individual stories into one through-line narrative. I agreed to have a go. Murry encouraged me not to worry too much about the budget.

The task proved to be tricky. A.A. Milne's classic book consists of several beautifully crafted stories, each with a satisfying beginning, middle and end. Each story employs a different combination of characters. Somehow I had to structure a continuous narrative while preserving the well-loved disparate incidents. Eventually I came up with the idea of a revolving stage enabling us to travel to various areas of the Hundred Acre Wood, linking scenes and characters without appearing to end one sequence and start another.

Murry and I spent several months corresponding across the Atlantic by email, and when she was happy with my detailed synopsis, she said that it would now be presented to the powers that be.

Eventually, Murry tearfully rang me. The producer had reacted with horror at the scale of my proposals, saying they would be far too expensive to put into operation. It came down to a debate about art versus commercialism and I knew which would win, so Disney decided not to run with my adaptation. Murry, showing considerable loyalty, resigned on the spot, saying that the whole point of her appointment had been to improve the quality of the arena shows, and that she was certain she had delivered exactly what was required.

I asked Murry what she was now going to do. She told me she hoped to run her own children's theatre company and that I would become its Patron, and that they would produce some of my plays. Within a few years, her ambition was realised. She set up the MainStreet Theatre Company based in the Lewis Family Playhouse, in Rancho Cucamonga, a city thirty-seven miles east of Downtown Los Angeles. I was delighted to be the Patron, and to also become a writer-in-residence for a short time. I gave storytelling sessions in the adjoining library and performed *David Wood's Storytime* in the theatre. For more than ten years Murry has regularly produced my plays, and our association has been a very warm one. Losing out on the Disney connection was a disappointment, but it led to a lasting friendship and professional relationship that I treasure.

For seven months, in 2005–6, I beavered away writing a play called *The Queen's Handbag*. This was quite unlike any of my previous commissions. It was unique. It was performed on a very large stage constructed in Buckingham Palace Gardens, directed by the legendary Trevor Nunn, and watched by eight million viewers on BBC television. The play was presented as part of the eightieth birthday celebrations of Her Majesty the Queen. The *Children's Party at the Palace*, attended by 2,000 children accompanied by 1,000 adults, was a Sunday-afternoon event celebrating British children's literature. The gardens were transformed into a theme park of attractions ranging from Captain Hook's pirate ship from *Peter Pan* on the lake to *Alice's Adventures in Wonderland*'s Mad Hatter's Tea Party on the terrace and a re-creation of *Winnie-the-Pooh*'s Hundred Acre Wood. The BBC asked me to write their contribution to the day's festivities, a play featuring as many great characters from British children's fiction as possible, all coming together to feature in one newly-written story. They wanted to capture the imagination of the children and simultaneously revive the childhood memories of the adults. This was an exciting project, a one-off opportunity to bring together the iconic creations of our country's greatest children's writers.

My storyline involved the Queen inviting the characters to the party. But baddies were not included. Taking umbrage at this slight, they plot to sabotage the party. Part of the plan is for Burglar Bill to steal the Queen's handbag, in which will be her reading glasses and the text of the speech she will be giving at the end. This idea was suggested by the fact that we knew that the Queen would in fact make an entrance at the end of the play, and praise our literary heritage and encourage children to love books.

Part of my brief was to help my BBC producers to enthuse the copyright holders of the characters involved and to encourage them to allow these characters to appear in the play, interacting with other characters. Given the special nature of this never-to-be-repeated occasion, and in the knowledge that considerable publicity for their publications was inevitable, the majority of copyright holders enthusiastically agreed to the proposal. But some expressed concerns. The Postman Pat people objected to the idea of their children's favourite being kidnapped by the baddies on his way to deliver invitations. And Chorion, who then looked after Noddy and Big Ears, having at first been enthusiastic about star names likes Keira Knightly and Robbie Coltrane playing the characters, suddenly asked for a meeting. They now didn't want star names, because they believed that children could only accept the Channel 5 versions of Noddy and Big Ears, the ones in which their heads resemble cartoon characters with non-human faces, rather like carnival heads. I said this could be possible, but when I described the scene in which Noddy and Big Ears were driving in Noddy's car to the party, it was pointed out that actors wearing such heads wouldn't be able to see well enough to drive. As a result, the scene was lost, and Noddy and Big Ears only appeared in a scene in a tube station.

A top executive from Disney in Los Angeles flew to London to discuss with me Winnie-the-Pooh's proposed appearance. Winnie-the-Pooh may be our most celebrated British children's character, but, as he is owned by Disney, we needed permission to include him. Taking the idea from the story of *Goldilocks*, I wanted the three bears – Winnie-the-Pooh, Paddington and Rupert – to search together for the Queen's handbag. The rights holders of Paddington and Rupert had agreed straightaway. But I was told that never in the history of Disney had any of their characters ever shared a scene with characters from another stable. I pointed out that this was the whole point. My idea was a one-off, part of our tribute to the Queen. The Disney executive was sympathetic, but said he would have to return to LA for high-level discussion. But he certainly wanted to support the project, and offered to send Glenn Close over in a private jet, complete with wardrobe and make-up people so she could appear as Cruella de Ville, her celebrated Disney role, from Dodie Smith's *One Hundred and One Dalmatians*. My BBC producer jumped on this offer, and I subsequently managed to write Cruella into the script. She wanted to come to the party at the Queen's home, in order to kidnap her corgis, with which to make herself a new fur coat. A couple of months later we were informed that Ms Close was not available. But Disney would be happy for Helen Mirren to play Cruella. However, Ms Mirren was not available. In the end, I'm pleased to say that Amanda Redman was splendid in the role.

Eventually we heard that, after serious debate, Disney would only allow Winnie-the-Pooh to be seen in the same shot as Paddington and Rupert, if Winnie-the-Pooh was first seen in a fenced-off part of the Hundred Acre Wood. Paddington and Rupert could approach the fence, look over, and in mime ask Winnie-the-Pooh if he had had any success looking for the handbag. Winnie-the-Pooh would shake his head, and the others move off. The implication was that doing it this way the Disney hero would not have been compromised by the non-Disney bears. And that is indeed how the scene was eventually shot.

Despite all of this frustrating and somewhat corporate approach to the project, it is only fair to record my deep admiration for the undeniable role Disney has played in the provision of quality family entertainment for nearly a century. Our lives have all been enriched by their timeless movies and their understanding of children. Their belief in the entitlement of children to their own genre of cinema has delivered a clutch of classics that will surely outlive the majority of films aimed solely at adult audiences.

PICTURE CREDITS

All images are from the author's personal collection, unless otherwise indicated.

Front cover: Richard Burton and Elizabeth Taylor – Angus McBean Photograph (MS Thr 581) © Harvard Theatre Collection, Houghton Library, Harvard University.

Dr Faustus: Faustus and Mephistophilis / Helen of Troy / Faustus with Students / When Hollywood Came to Oxford – Angus McBean Photograph (MS Thr 581) © Harvard Theatre Collection, Houghton Library, Harvard University.

The Vamp: Shelley Winters and me © ITV/Shutterstock.

Jeeves: Cast Photo / In my tennis shorts / A staged farewell – Photographs by Lichfield.

Aces High: The Team Photo / Me in my flying jacket / 2nd Lt. Croft (Peter Firth) and 2nd Lt. 'Tommy' Thompson – Courtesy of STUDIOCANAL.

North Sea Hijack: Me with Anthony Perkins / My close-up masterclass – Courtesy of Universal Studios Licensing LLC.

The Queen's Handbag: The stage and audience in Buckingham Palace Gardens / Tracy Beaker returns the handbag to the Queen / The Queen, reunited with her handbag, is pleased to find her speech – Photographs by Ian Jones.